MARK CULLEN

THE COMPLETE GARDENER

COLOUR & DESIGN

W9-BJE-684

Ballantine Books

Ballantine Books
A division of Random House of Canada Limited
1265 Aerowood Drive
Mississauga, ON L4W 1B9

INFACT Publishing Ltd.
66 Portland St., 2nd Floor
Toronto, ON M5V 2M8

CTV Television Network Ltd.
250 Yonge St., 18th Floor
Toronto, ON M5B 2N8

Canadian Cataloguing in Publication Data

Cullen, Mark, 1956—
      Colour & design
(Mark Cullen's Complete gardener series)
Accompanied by video.
Includes index.
ISBN 0-345-39830-0

1. Gardens — Design. 2. Colour in gardening. I. Title.
II. Title: Colour and design. III. Series: Cullen, Mark,
1956— . Mark Cullen's Complete gardener series.

SB473.C85 1996   712'.6   C96-930030-1

PHOTOS: Janet Davis—p. 17, 18, 29, 39, 40, 42, 57, 63, 71,
    75, 77, 84, 87, 89, 91; Ted Johnston—p. 8, 30, 34
SENIOR EDITOR: Wendy Thomas
HORTICULTURAL EDITOR: Denis Flanagan
COPY EDITOR: Sylvia Gilchrist
CTV CO-ORDINATOR: Glen Dickout, Manager, Special Projects
PROJECT MANAGER: Susan Yates, INFACT Publishing
COVER AND TEXT DESIGN AND ILLUSTRATION ART: ArtPlus:
    Brant Cowie, Dave Murphy and Jerry Stapley
SPECIAL THANKS: Dan Matheson, Canada am; Jean and John
    Farintosh; Aunt Charlotte and Uncle Tom; Len Cullen,
    my Dad; and especially, Mary for her help and support.

M+M Communications, Unionville, ON is the publishing imprint of Mary and Mark Cullen.

Printed and bound in Canada by Metropole Litho Inc.

TABLE OF CONTENTS

· ·

INTRODUCTION

"What exactly do you do?" I am sometimes asked, in reference to my "day job." My response to that is to suggest that my professional goal in life is to remove the hocus-pocus, or the barriers, that Canadians imagine stand between them and success in the garden.

This book and video are a natural extension of what I do with great passion every day. My intent is to show you how to get the most out of your garden and to do it by minimizing the "work" (maintenance) and maximizing what I believe to be the most pleasurable aspects of gardening, including lounging around the yard in a favourite chair or hammock.

My good friend Dan Matheson is no gardening dummy. Truth is, he is a fast learner with more enthusiasm than most of us can imagine. He also has a habit of asking the very questions that Canadian gardeners (and non gardeners!) have on their minds at the time. I think you will enjoy this book and video as we simplify gardening and help you to get the most from your Canadian garden through *The Complete Gardener.*

The issues of colour and design are tricky ones for many gardeners — beginners and experienced alike. I hope you find that this book tells you the fundamentals, with some useful tips and advice, to give you the confidence to make your garden the place of beauty of which you dream.

MARK CULLEN

GARDEN STYLES

· · · · · · · · · · · · · · · · · ·

The art of gardening has a wonderful history. It began when human beings ceased their nomadic ways and started living a settled, agricultural life. The purpose of the first gardens was to provide food. A garden was often dedicated to the gods as it was believed that the gods would give life to the garden and create fruits and flowers. From early gardens in Egypt, Babylon, Persia, and Greece, garden concepts evolved as agricultural techniques improved.

Over the centuries, different regions and cultures became noted for particular styles of gardening. For example, Egyptian gardens used water as an important element, for irrigation as well as for fish ponds. In Persia, gardens were enclosed by walls to separate them from the wild desert and to provide shade and coolness. They, too, used water channels, often arranged in terraces, around which the rest of the garden was designed. The Romans' influence was profoundly felt because of the reach of their empire. Perhaps the best known from that time is Hadrian's Villa, a large country estate built by the Emperor Hadrian between AD 118 and

Courtyards surrounded by covered breezeways have a Mediterranean feel.

138. It had a great influence on future similar extravagant gardens for its use of monuments, buildings, and motifs that recalled past glories or other parts of the world.

While most Canadian gardens don't recall glories of the past to the same extent as European or Eastern gardens, our gardens do show direct links to the past, even though we might not be aware of it. For example, the first patio was created by the Muslims at the beginning of the eighth century in southern Spain. When we plan formal gardens with carefully clipped hedges and symmetrical layouts, we are recreating, in our own small way, the great Renaissance gardens that had their beginnings in Italy around the middle of the fifteenth century.

The gardens most like our own are the ones that came about during the early nineteenth century, when gardening changed once again. At that time, one of the most profound gardening inventions appeared on the scene: the lawn mower. Not surprisingly, it was invented by an Englishman, Edwin Beard Budding, who patented it in August 1830. Up until then, only wealthy landowners could keep their vast lawns cut, for they had the resources to hire a team of gardeners who would scythe the grass. This was also the century when garden fashion turned from formal, geometric patterns to more natural plantings, culminating in the work in Britain of Gertrude Jekyll who refined the herbaceous border.

Today, we carry on the great traditions of gardening as we plan and plant our gardens. As in the past, the style of our houses influences the style of our gardens; therefore, garden fashions of the past are not always appropriate to the buildings of today. It is not necessary to follow exactly the elements that made, for example, the classical garden or the English cottage garden; but, if you know some of the recognized garden styles of the past, you can adapt these styles to your own conditions and situation.

MEADOW GARDEN

The meadow garden is variously described as natural or wild but no such thing as a 'wild' garden can exist and truly be called a garden. A garden is by definition controlled in some fashion by the gardener. To me, a meadow garden is attractive and interesting under certain circumstances — when you have the space, where you want low maintenance, where some foot traffic occurs, and where you want to create a look that changes constantly throughout the gardening season. In a meadow garden you can expect a range of colours from the rich, bright colours of the summer months to the grey, brown hues of late autumn.

❀ Wild gardens were in vogue in the late nineteenth century as a reaction to the formality and ostentation of the Victorian period. However, even in those times, the garden areas around the house retained their culti-vated characteristics. Today, meadow — or native or wild — gardens are more a means for the gardener to explore an interest in native plants and conservation.

❀ Meadow gardens usually look best from a distance and are often more appropriate on country or cottage properties. They can make a good transition between the garden and wilder parts of the landscape. The meadow garden should be mowed once a year in the late summer, after most plants have set seeds.

❀ Suggested plantings: wild grasses, bulbs, wildflower mixes. If you purchase a wildflower mix, be sure there are both annual and perennial seeds in it. It can take a couple of years for the perennials to get established and the annuals can fill in during that time. Look for wildflowers that are native to your region and use them in your meadow garden.

A country property or cottage is the home for a meadow garden.

PARTERRE DESIGN

This stylized type of bedding or grouping of similar plants grew out of knot gardens and is a geometric, ornamental arrangement of shaped beds that are separated from one another by paths or grassed areas.

❀ The pattern is outlined by formal trimmed hedges. Inside, the pattern may be filled by grass or flowers. Annuals make better fillers because of their continuous bloom, providing colour throughout the season. Some appropriate materials for planting the outlines are dwarf box (the traditional plant for this purpose), yew, santolina, or lavender.

❀ An example of parterre is a grouping of four beds arranged symmetrically around a central ornamental feature. The beds form a complete pattern; if any were to be removed, the pattern would be destroyed.

❀ Other possibilities for filling the interior of the hedged area: gravel; water; vegetables; herbs; a mixture of shrubs and perennials.

❀ This type of garden does not offer the opportunity to grow a wide variety of plants but is undertaken for the precision of its lines, the contrasts of colours that can be used, and the way it relates to its accompanying buildings.

This parterre is outlined by a trimmed hedge. The interior is a mix of shrubs and perennials.

9

ITALIAN STYLE GARDEN

The Italian style garden is also called Italian Renaissance style. These gardens incorporate the best of gardening from Egypt, Syria, Babylon, Greece, and the Classic Roman style.

❉ The gardens are architectural in character, for they are closely related to the villas, casinos, and palaces around which they were constructed. Often, they were located on hillsides, where they could take advantage of magnificent views.

❉ These gardens use water lavishly — in cascades, fountains, and pools. On the other hand, plant material is used in a restrained fashion — hedges of box or yew, very little grass, large gravel areas, and virtually no perennial flowers.

❉ Colour is supplied by climbing roses, pots of annuals, and, sometimes, parterre patterns of bedding plants.

❉ Evergreens are used but very few leafy shrubs or deciduous trees.

❉ Other elements, such as walls, stairways, and statuary, are fanciful and large.

FRENCH STYLE

Traditional French gardens are an adaptation of the Italian. Their sites were usually less rugged than the Italians had to contend with.

❉ The French used parterre beds as well, but made the designs more ornate and elaborate. Their sculptures and other ornamentation were more fanciful and romantic but smaller in scale. Water was not used as much and grass replaced gravel.

❉ Trellis work, wall decorations, and garden pavilions were used by the French.

CLASSICAL FORMAL STYLE

Symmetry, simplicity, and repetition, either in plants or furnishings, are important aspects of the design of the classical garden. The strictly formal garden presents an axis, both sides of which are mirror images or identical.

✤ In a classical garden, the structure is designed to be pleasing. The bones of the garden are clear and the design qualities are often more important than the plantings. Whether the plantings are colourful, romantic, and unrestrained or contained, minimal, and quiet, they are always seen in relation to the design as a whole.

✤ The structure of the garden is made up of walls, hedges, paths, and sculpture, and enhanced by plants chosen for their shape, colour, and texture. This "hard landscape" often has an aged look to it, something that can be difficult to mimic in Canada, so approach this type of design with some caution. Most classical gardens are made over years, not over a weekend or even a season. The walls and paths age naturally along with the rest of the garden. Classical gardens, with their strong architectural elements, look especially attractive in the winter covered with snow — a bonus for the Canadian gardener.

✤ Water may be still, running, or run through a fountain.

✤ Plantings are often masses of similar varieties rather than the riot of a cottage garden.

✤ Classical garden design lends itself readily to the use of a focal point, such as an urn, a sundial, a statue, or a well-placed garden bench. These elements often take pride of place over a plant specimen — it's as if the purpose of the plant is to show off the structure, rather than the structure acting as a backdrop for the plants.

ENGLISH COTTAGE GARDEN

An English cottage garden is the ideal of many gardeners. When we got married, I had to promise Mary that we would have what she refers to as a "messy" garden — an English cottage garden! In Canada, it is difficult to recreate the soft misty air that seems a part of the English landscape but we can certainly use some of the traditional plants. Most of us don't live in the perfect accompaniment to the cottage garden — a thatched cottage! But many older Canadian houses, from urban bungalows to country farmhouses, look right at home with this garden style.

❀ Historically, a cottage garden in England was the garden of the "humbler" folk. Paths were made of local materials, were relatively narrow, and had a practical purpose. Gates were simple and usually made of wood rather than metal. Fences were rustic in nature and often hedges were used to keep farm animals out and to mark the change from garden to surrounding countryside. The plantings were usually chosen because they were useful (food, medicine, dyes) or because they were admired by the gardener. Plantings were often random, but nevertheless charming.

❀ To recreate the feel of an English cottage garden, trees should be fruit or nut trees — apple, plum, pear, cherry, hazel, almond. Holly or yew are appropriate evergreens.

❀ Lawns in a cottage garden are not large. Such open spaces in the original English country garden would have been given over to a vegetable patch.

❀ Colourful plants, including herbs such as chives, parsley, bergamot, lemon balm, and thyme, in simple containers by the front door are appropriate in this relaxed and unpretentious design.

The English cottage garden: a joyful and abundant variety of colour, shape, and height.

❀ Incorporate vegetables and fruit bushes into the design for a feeling of total harmony. Herbaceous perennials are the backbone of the cottage garden: foxgloves, hollyhocks, peonies, daisies, lupines, stocks, delphiniums, and irises.

❀ Scented plants, such as lavender and scented geraniums, are right at home in the cottage garden, as are climbing roses and honeysuckles.

❀ The effect you are seeking is one of a rich profusion of flowers — and they don't have to be only the old-fashioned favourites. Let them run together in bold enthusiastic bunches. They can tumble into the paths and over edges of retaining walls or containers.

❀ Arbours, trellises, and furniture should all be of a simple or even rustic nature. Wood and stone are more appropriate materials than concrete or metal.

VICTORIAN STYLE

Victorians were passionately interested in scientific discovery and the cultivation of plants from far-away. They took seriously the collection and display of new plant specimens. Gardens, like so much else in Victorian times, became formal and ostentatious. Sheer quantity counted but, unlike the cottage garden, there is a great sense of order in the plantings. Beds were carved out of lawns and brightly planted.

❁ Weeping trees were favoured, but many other trees were clipped. Roses were extremely popular.

❁ The lawn was the pride and glory of the garden. Grass was close-shaven and carefully maintained. In Canada, we can only hope to have the equivalent of an English lawn with its fine creeping emerald-green blades. If you desire a garden in the Victorian style, be prepared to pamper your lawn. The edgings must be precise and perfect.

❁ The Victorian garden is rich in detail and rather formal. It has been described as "ostentatiously gardened." Shrubs are well clipped, edges are clearly defined, and there is a general feeling of controlled abundance.

❁ Columns, urns, formal outdoor vases on pedestals, intricate ironwork, formal fountains — any combination will give the feel of a Victorian garden. Can you overdo it? Probably not. Just think of Victorian interiors which are full of fussy and crowded detail.

❁ Get out the white paint and use it lavishly — on fences, arbours, benches, chairs, and especially anything made of wrought iron.

❁ This type of garden can be time-consuming to maintain. In the Victorian era, labour was cheap. Not so today. A Victorian garden, though, can become a labour of love and many low-maintenance building materials, such as vinyl, substitute nicely for the high maintenance of wood.

JAPANESE STYLE

A Japanese style garden is, above all, a place of tranquillity. Traditionally, every element has been symbolic of some aspect of nature or human life. Today, the symbolism is less important, but the elements are still used because of their traditional and aesthetic connections.

✿ The Japanese garden is restrained, full of contrasts of light and shade, and hard and soft textures. Each element is placed so that it looks natural in the landscape and seems to have been there forever. The idea is to suggest nature, rather than copy it, a practice that makes it well-suited to small spaces.

✿ Water is one of the most important elements in a Japanese garden. Used in waterfalls and water courses, it is meant to suggest high mountain streams. Bridges and stone lanterns are used as symbols of a safe pathway. When water is not gently flowing in the Japanese garden, it is still. Fountains are not used.

✿ If water is not present, it is suggested by flowing white sand, gravel, or small stones. The impression of waves is created by raking these materials. Boulders often emerge from these constructed rivers, and stepping stones, both in real and implied streams, are often used.

✿ The other important elements in this garden are stone and greenery. Flowers do not play an important part, but when they are used, they are likely to be irises, peonies, lilies, or chrysanthemums.

✿ Stones or boulders are arranged in groups to represent mountains; flat stones can form a path.

✿ Stone lanterns are placed by paths or bridges to give light to the visitor. Bridge railings and screens are frequently constructed of bamboo.

✸ Straight lines are not usually found in a Japanese garden. Walls are rarely used. Separating one part of the garden from the other or separating the garden from the street or next door is achieved by using fences of bamboo or screens of grasses.

✸ Common plants in a Japanese garden are plum, cherry, Japanese maple, yews, and bamboo. Pines and juniper may be clipped into floating cloud shapes. As well, rhododendrons and azaleas fit into the feeling very nicely. If your climate is accommodating, moss can be used as a "floor." All plant material is used sparingly.

MODERN GARDEN

The modern garden takes its inspiration from modern architecture. It uses clean, hard landscaping materials and fewer plants than in most other styles of gardens.

✸ The plants exhibit architectural qualities and are chosen more for their form and texture than their flowers. They have clean lines and bold foliage that contrasts with other plants or with the other garden features.

✸ Water in a symmetrically shaped pool is used to good advantage in a modern garden. It adds another dimension but is frequently left unadorned by plantings. Plant material that is used tends to have strong architectural qualities.

✸ Hard furnishing materials, such as marble, slate, interlocking brick, and concrete, can be used for paths, patios, and tabletops. Wood, as long as it is not rustic, can be used in many situations in the modern garden.

✸ Ideas from the classical gardens and minimalist elements from Japanese gardens can be introduced into

The modern garden uses texture, shape, and restrained colour to achieve its beauty.

the modern garden without being jarring, but the busy nature of an English cottage garden would be out of place.

Clear lines, whether straight or curving, are the hall-mark of the modern garden. Trellises, arbours, tables, and chairs should be simple in design.

Because of its uncluttered nature, the modern style is suited to small areas, such as courtyards.

Cacti, with their unusual forms and textures, make good additions to the modern garden. In our Canadian climate, grow them in containers and bring them indoors in the winter.

Ground covers are not plants but gravel, square or rectangular stones, or large slabs of cement. These can be used in conjunction with parterre plantings.

* Abstract or modern sculpture makes an effective focal point in a modern garden.

* Modern gardens are appropriate for houses with clean lines and little ornamentation, such as shutters. The bold simple lines of the house should be carried through to the garden.

CANADIAN STYLE

Is there a Canadian style? I would say yes, but it cannot be codified as have been the preceding styles. The Canadian 'style' is evolving. For me, it is a reflection of our culture and, therefore, is as varied as the people who make up our fascinating and diverse country.

* The Canadian style borrows from all of the previously mentioned styles, then throws in a dash of

Bright colour in the late summer Canadian garden.

whimsy, outrageousness, inventiveness, and individuality.

❋

As Canadians we work with our particular micro-climates and zones; sometimes we push the limits of our plants' endurance — we tempt fate by putting out the pansies earlier and earlier every year.

❋

We keep up the traditions started by our forebears when they came to this country, but we blend large native trees and rocks into our landscape to create a rustic appearance that reflects our natural landscape.

❋

You can design and create a garden that fits any of the descriptions offered in this chapter; but, if it includes the use of native plants and natural features, it must, by definition, be Canadian.

PLANNING YOUR DREAM LANDSCAPE

W hat do you see when you look out over your yard? Chances are that the sight falls short of the dream landscape you have in your mind's eye. To accomplish your dream landscape, you need to know some of the basics of landscape design, some of which you may already know intuitively. You must also understand your vision and be prepared to make it change as time goes by.

It is not hard for you to become a gardener who feels that it is possible to develop a gorgeous landscape. First, you must remember that although there are some "rules" in gardening to follow, there are no rules that can't be broken. Second, you should understand some principles of design and gardening before setting out to break them. We'll look at some of the basics of design in Chapter 3. Be realistic about your garden — that hard compromise between what you have to work with and what you want your garden to be. Above all, the garden should reflect your own interests and dreams, not those of someone else.

USE OF YOUR YARD

To be brutally honest about how you use your yard may be the hardest part of coming up with your garden design. You must consider not how you would like to use your yard, but how you actually use it. You might dream of an English cottage garden, but if you have small children, those foxgloves are going to be trampled pretty quickly. If you have a young family, your uses of the garden over the next ten years or so will change. The garden will go from a play area to an entertaining area; perhaps a swimming pool will replace the jungle gym; eventually the swimming pool will disappear to be replaced by your English country garden. So, to the best extent possible, take into account how you can accommodate future desires with your current needs. When you prepare your wish lists, write three: one for the garden you desire today, another for ten years from now, and another for twenty years.

Now for the practical considerations. Make a list of what you want in your garden and what you need in the garden. Below, I have listed some questions you should ask yourself as you ponder the ways in which your garden is or will be used. Some of these are elements or uses often found in a garden, and some are features that look good and which you might want to incorporate into your design. It is unlikely that you will be able to implement your garden plans in one season, so identify the ones that are the most important and do those first. Perhaps they will be the least expensive parts of the plan; however, if construction is involved, you may have to make it your priority. Everything else will then be able to go in around the construction.

❋ *Who uses the garden and what do they use it for?*

This question should be answered before any others. It will help you answer all the others that follow. If this is your first garden, I suggest you take a year — that's right, a year! — before you come to any hard and fast ideas about your garden, especially about the private part of the garden, usually the "back yard." The public garden, the front yard, is often used less frequently as recreational space. Even if this isn't your first garden, waiting for a year will let you observe your site in changing weathers and seasons. You will be able to see how shadows are cast at different times of the year; if there are spots protected from or exposed to wind and sun; if there are drainage problems; and, if you have inherited a garden, what is already planted. Over the year note how the garden and the house are used by various family members, pets, and visitors. How do people get from the garage to the house? Do people take a shortcut across the front lawn? Do visitors come to the front door, the back door, the side door? Are you going to need more parking space someday?

❋ *Do you need to provide a place for your children to play?*

Try to situate the play area so that it is visible from the house. Plan to use a soft bark mulch under swings, slides, and other play areas to cushion the inevitable tumbles. Consider building a toy box in which to store outdoor toys.

❋ *Do you want a garden structure such as a gazebo, arbour, pergola, deck, verandah, or porch added to the house?*

A gazebo makes a good focal point and is a nice place to relax. Arbours and pergolas can lead you along a path to a nicely presented chair or a secret part of the garden. Decks, verandahs, and porches provide places to entertain, relax, and undertake small gardening chores. For more information on garden structures, refer to *The Complete Gardener, Furnishings* book.

Do you entertain outdoors frequently and how many people do you entertain at one time?

Seating is an important item to work into your plan — in fact, it goes hand in hand with the previous question and the following question about barbecuing. Are there sheltered spots for sitting outdoors so that the beauty of the garden can be appreciated even in a light drizzle?

Is barbecuing an important part of your life?

Be honest about how much time you actually spend barbecuing. A barbecue area can be quite splendid with built-in counters and storage units. When drawing up your plans, combine the barbecue area with a dining area so the chef isn't isolated, and be careful not to place the barbecue near a neighbour's windows.

Do you need a place for a dog run?

If you have a dog, you may prefer to fence an area of your garden so that your dog can be outside with-

A small home lends itself to simplicity in landscape design.

out ruining your lawns and flowerbeds. If you use strong chainlink fencing, which is not particularly attractive, you can mask it with vines or shrubs, which will also provide shade for the dog.

Is a swimming pool or hot tub a desired addition to your garden?

A swimming pool will likely need to be fenced. Situate it in a sunny spot so it will be used more frequently. Think of incorporating it into the rest of the landscape naturally. The soil removed for an in-ground pool can be used to construct a berm elsewhere in the garden to vary the elevations in the garden or to build the base of a rock garden. If a hot tub is in the plans, you will probably want to situate it near the house for convenience.

How much time do you want to spend gardening?

This may seem like an odd question, but some people who want to have a garden don't enjoy gardening. They see the garden as a place for the pool, the hot tub, the barbecue, the patio, and so forth. A few shrubs and some containers fulfil their desire to garden. There is nothing wrong with this — just be honest about it.

How important is having and maintaining a lawn?

A lawn area is one of the most flexible and least expensive elements to install in your garden. There are many options to lawns — ground covers and paving are just two — but a lawn can add great beauty to a garden. It makes a lovely smooth green canvas for shadows to play across during the day; it cools the air; and it is soft on the feet. Above all, a lawn bears up better than anything else to foot traffic.

Do you want to grow vegetables or have a herb garden?

A vegetable bed needs lots of sun, but you don't need a large area. Many vegetables can be trained up frames (beans and peas are just two), and miniature vegetables have been developed for container growing and small beds (try sweet one million cherry tomatoes). Herb gardens need sun and well-drained soil. If space is limited, herbs do well in containers.

❄ *What other special gardens might you like? Water garden? Rock garden? Rose garden?*

Water gardens are best situated away from large trees. If small children are around, safety is a concern with a water garden. Any excavated soil can be used to build up another part of the garden or to create a rock garden. Rock gardens need to be positioned in a sunny, well-drained spot (minimum six hours per day). Rose gardens require a sunny area.

❄ *Are you a plant collector?*

If your gardening interests run to collecting particular specimens, growing rare plants from seeds, or indulging a passion for a particular species or variety, your garden will be laid out with very different considerations. Your concerns will be with displaying your prized specimens to their best advantage and possibly with providing working space in your garden. A lathe house will give shade and some shelter and act as a place to store tools and equipment on a temporary basis.

❄ *Do you want a garden that is attractive to birds?*

Planting and furnishing a garden that attracts birds brings movement and interest to the garden. If this is one of your objectives, ask a neighbourhood bird enthusiast about the birds in your area and seek out the plants that they prefer.

❄ *Is there a dry, secure place to keep garden tools? If not, will you build one? Where will it be located?*

You may already own an arsenal of gardening equipment; if so, this question will be answered pretty quickly as you try to find space for them. Consider combining a tool shed with a potting shed, especially if space is at a limit.

Narrow Lot

Long narrow lots are typical in many Canadian subdivisions. In this makeover, three distinct areas have been fashioned: front, side, and back yards. Shrubs planted along the driveway to the entry lead the eye to the front door. The walk from the driveway has been widened to soften the entrance and distinguish it from similar houses. A small shrub has been removed to put down paving material that joins front and back yards and extends around the decking. A new tree frames the front and provides privacy in the rest of the yard. The sides are planted with shrubs. In the back, a border has been added that extends under the tree for shade-loving plants. An island bed has been added — it could be used as a rock garden or water garden.

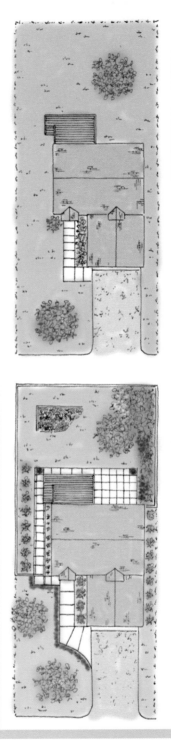

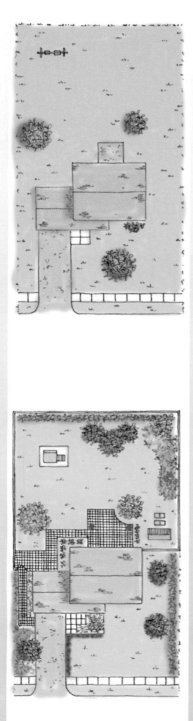

Typical Lot

Another urban lot that can easily be planted to separate the public and private parts. Trees on either side of the house frame it, aided by new plantings down both sides of the lot. Paving unites back to front visually but a fence and gate make it clear that the visitor is entering the private part of the garden. Existing trees are incorporated into the new design and a new grove is added at the back. These three trees create a soft focal point viewed from the new patio and the house. There's still a lot of lawn for kids to run around on, and the flowerbeds are set off in their own room, with a utility area tucked neatly away, hidden from the patio by a planting of shrubs.

❀ ....

Is composting an important gardening activity for you?
(To me it is!)

The position of the composter in your garden
is important. Well-composted material normally
doesn't smell, but people still seem to like to place
the composter as far away from the house as possible. Wherever you place it, the location should be
convenient for at least one of its uses — either it
should be easy to get to from the house, or it should
be near the place where the finished compost will be
used. Can you get to it in the winter? All winter you
can be adding peels from your veggies and fruits so
that they will be ready to start breaking down when
the warm weather comes. Have you got space for
more than one bin? This will make you the envy of
all your composting friends! Can you place one near
the house for winter use?

❀ ....

Where will watering and lighting fixtures be placed?
Should existing ones be moved?

If you are undergoing serious outdoor construction, this is the time to install an inground watering
system and increase your lighting fixtures and elec-
trical outlets.

THE SITE — "MUST HAVE, NICE TO HAVE"

The next step is to look at what you've got and
assess how well it fits in with your needs and
desires. Certain aspects of the site are not flexible
— you can't change the direction the house faces,
the neighbours' tall hedge, or a windy exposure —
but there are ways of accommodating your design
to any perceived flaw. Decide what you can adapt,
what you absolutely cannot live with, and what is
on a short-term reprieve. Don't be too hasty to

In your design, include places to sit. This nook invites you to come and stay awhile.

get rid of large elements, such as trees. By pruning undergrowth or surrounding shrubs, a large tree can take on a whole new importance. By the time you have finished this assessment, you are bound to have added more items to your "must have, nice to have" list.

❀ Take the dimensions of the garden. Even if you don't draw a plan (see Chapter 3), you should know the size of your property. If decks or porches are to be built, you will need to know how much space they will take up. It will also give you a realistic idea of how many "rooms" you can divide your garden into. If your garden is small, start thinking of space-saving tricks, such as using trellises and hanging baskets for added colour.

❀ The shape of the garden and the relation of the garden to the house are two of the virtually unchangeable elements of the site. If you feel they are also the biggest problem, rise to the occasion and turn them to your advantage. Pore through gardening books and magazines; talk to neighbourhood gardeners. There isn't a gardening problem that can't be solved — but don't expect to have a successful rock garden on the damp north side of the house. In this battle of wills, Mother Nature will win. Learn to work with her, not against her. Just another word about shape — one of the hardest shapes to work with is a square, especially a small square. In such a situation, stay away from straight lines as much as possible. Beds should be curved and flowing. A deep bed along one side will soon get rid of the "square-box" feeling.

The *topography* of the garden will dictate the design to a large extent. An ideal site has interesting, gradual changes but most lots are not large enough to accommodate even one level of change. If you do have a sloping site, you can have fun deciding how you are going to get from one level to the next — you can find nearly any kind of material for paths and steps to suit your house and garden. The opposite end of the extreme, a flat site, can be as difficult to deal with. It can be made interesting by building a

A workshed carries through a theme: the intricate woodwork of the door, the unpretentious bench and quaint bird houses, the rustic basket, the glossy milk can — all show a unity of purpose.

berm with topsoil; breaking the garden up with
flowerbeds, hedges, or fences; installing raised beds;
using plants to provide varying heights; or making a
path whose end is not visible at its beginning.

❊ Do any walls, fences, and hedges, exist already? Are
they a problem or an advantage? Do they act as a
windbreak (think twice before getting rid of these
features — they may have a very practical reason for
existing there)? Are walls eyesores? Cover them with
vines or tall plants. Do fences need replacing? Talk
to your neighbour before replacing them. It is not
only good manners but you may be able to work out
a way to split the cost of replacement.

❊ Is there a view from the house or the garden that
must be maintained — a view that will cause delight
to everyone who looks at it? Start to think about
how it can be framed by plantings and how the eye
will be directed to it from several parts of the house
and garden.

❊ Assess your soil. Is it sand, clay, or perfect garden
loam? Buy a soil-test kit at a garden centre to measure its pH. Take a soil sample in for a test and ask
how best to improve your soil. These two exercises
will help you choose the plants you can grow.

❊ Where is it sunny and for how long? Is there perpet-
ual shade in a particular spot of the garden? Is it a
heavy and constant shade caused by a building or is
it shade thrown by a grove of trees? If the shade is
caused by trees, you have several options if you want
to increase the sun coming into your garden. The
most drastic, of course, is to remove a tree. Another
option is to thin the branches. Not only will thin-
ning introduce more light and air movement into
the garden, but it will probably make the tree more
attractive. Is there a corner of your garden that
warms up quickly in the spring and stays warm in
the late fall? Such little sun traps can be attractive

corners in the spring, so try to work in a small bed for spring bulbs.

✳ Where does the prevailing wind come from? If you live in a coastal area, it is easy to tell by the direction in which the bushes and trees lean. Have wind tunnels been formed between two houses or in an alley between a house and garage. Wind causes plants to lose their moisture and can stunt and deform growth if it is relentless. The best windbreaks are those that filter or reduce the wind. Many plants, such as fast-growing evergreens like spruce, pine cedar, are good, permanent windbreaks. Trellis screens can also be used for a quick fix.

✳ Unless you are buying a new house, you will probably inherit plants and features from the previous owner. Again, my advice is to go slow. Prune, yes. Weed, yes. Water and cultivate. But ponder before you do a full-scale renovation. In spite of that, remember there are no rules that can't be broken. If you really dislike your new garden and can't bear the thought of having to wait before you make a change, tear it out and start again. Be warned — you could be getting rid of some lovely old plants. If you don't want them, offer them to your local horticultural society or your neighbours.

✳ Finally, assess the style of your house. You want to enhance your house with the plants you grow and the outdoor furnishings. Be sure they carry through the character of your house. With a newer house, this can be difficult.

RULE OF THUMB:

Take pictures. A picture is "worth a thousand words" when describing your needs to a professional at a garden centre.

BASICS OF DESIGN

....

DESIGN PRINCIPLES

What is the best way to approach garden design? I say: You have some alternatives. If it helps you to put things down on paper, use grid paper and coloured pencils to chart your plantings over the seasons. When you use this method, you need to be able to visualize how the garden will look from ground level. Another method is to actually go out in the garden and use a hose or rope to lay out the forms of beds. Use your imagination about the plantings while still at this planning stage. Look at the proposed beds from all angles, including from the house. And if you are a high-tech gardener, computer programs are on the market to help you with your design.

What makes good design? There is no definitive answer. Just as beauty is in the eye of the beholder, so is good design. If you have a dream of what you want your garden to be and just can't seem to get it right, it is handy to understand some of the basic principles of design. Use them as a checklist to see if you can isolate where you think you may have gone off the tracks, but don't feel you have to adhere to them exactly. Like an artist, you will be creating a mood by using such design techniques as colour, line, form, scale, texture. Also, like an artist, you will throw the rules to the wind when something just feels right to you. Study plantings in books, visit botanical gardens, or go on garden tours to observe first hand how different gardens are laid out and how texture, contrast, and colour are used. It is a great way to see what works and doesn't work without spending a lot of money!

Here are some of my favourite principles to keep in mind while you plan your landscape.

A fence cuts through a flowerbed at an intriguing angle to separate two parts of a garden.

Rooms

One of the easiest ways to get started on garden design is to transfer to the outdoors the way you approach decorating indoors. The interior of your house is already divided into rooms and, even in open-concept houses, there are areas designated as places for eating, cooking, bathing, sleeping, entertaining, and so forth.

Think of your garden and the outdoor areas as either one big room or a series of small rooms. Consider developing a "living room," a play area, a work area, and so on. Employing this technique of imagining rooms will enable you to increase the use you get from your garden. Your property has probably already been divided into at least front and back rooms — your front and back yards. The front yard is the public face of the property. Make an effort to use plantings that complement the style of house you live in and reflect your lifestyle.

The style of garden you have in mind can be reflected in the way you lay out these outdoor rooms. Rooms for a formal garden are often rectangular in shape but can also be round or oval. Fences and hedges are used to clearly define them. The ground is usually level but if your lot slopes, terracing it would be in keeping with the formal feeling. In an informal design, rooms are less clearly defined and beds of shrubbery, ground covers, or even berms of earth can mark divisions.

Fences and hedges make great dividers, but flowerbeds can provide the necessary separation between two parts of the garden. If your yard is small, rooms can be separated by something as unobtrusive as a low box hedge or a rock garden. Did you know that a small garden can appear to be made larger by dividing it in half? This is a perfect way to apply the rooms' idea. You are getting increased use from your yard and you are making it appear larger. In all but the very smallest yard you can usually find a corner for a small water garden, a sandbox, a herb garden, or a shady corner with a comfortable chair.

Other good dividers are arbours and trellises that become "doorways" and serve two purposes: as a transition and as an opportunity for growing vines and climbers. However you choose to divide your garden, be sure that each room has a purpose so that the visitor or gardener feels welcome.

The "hallways" — the narrow side yards or alleys between houses — can be put to use, as well. Foliage plants with interesting texture can be used in shady spots but don't feel you have to rely only on plants to decorate these sometimes lost spaces. Paving material that links front and back will give a feeling of unity. Interesting pieces of sculpture, big or small, or strategically placed rocks and boulders can all enliven an otherwise forgotten area of the garden.

Another room often forgotten is the equivalent of the indoor mud room, workroom, or basement — that place where we store all the things we can't bear to throw out, where we repair household items, or store the less attractive items that keep a household going. Outdoors, the garbage bins, the dog run, the compost area, perhaps even a place for drying clothes are things or areas that you will want to include in your design.

You can conceal and enclose these rather unsightly necessities by using hedges, trellises, and fences. A hedge or trellis will do double duty by hiding the offending view and by being attractive in itself. When adding these necessities to your design, leave enough room for comfortable access or these areas will never be used properly.

A hedge used for screening can create a peaceful green background for other plantings or give the eye a rest from a close-by lively planting. An evergreen hedge offers year-round screening. A trellis can provide support for a flowering vine or one with interesting foliage. Provide variety by using a fast-growing annual vine such as morning glory instead of a perennial covering. If year-round covering of the trellis is important, use an evergreen vine such as euonymus. Fences also offer the opportunity to grow vines and climbers, while concealing what lies behind. The fence itself can become a special feature as long as it is very successful in completely hiding its secret — the material, the colour, the pattern, can all add to the

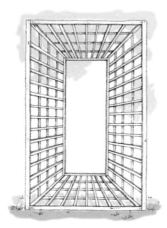

Trellises can be left unadorned rather than covered in vines. This one is designed as a trompe l'oeil focal point — it's an optical illusion that makes a space seem larger than it really is and livens up a dull wall.

interest of the fence, diverting attention even more successfully away from what's behind it. If you have inherited a chainlink fence, or decide you need a strong enclosure for a dog or vegetable garden, dress it up using a twining vine or plant shrubs, a hedge, or tall plants in front of it.

BACKGROUND

Walls in our houses provide an enclosure for our living space, privacy, shelter from the elements, and a background for our furniture and personal items. The walls of your outdoor room can do the same.

Walls, fences, hedges, shrubs, and trees act as windbreaks, enclosing and defining the garden and the various parts of it; they make the background against which to display plants and garden furnishings. This backdrop exists to show off your plantings and furnishings, so it should be peaceful and not draw attention to itself. It can hide unattractive sights and help focus attention on the delights of the garden. It should never overwhelm the rooms it contains.

PATHS

Even if you are not going to make a true path, there must be some way of travelling about your garden, of getting from the indoor house to the outdoor room or rooms. The path, especially if it is a curved path, is often what tempts the eye to put the feet in action. It moves you around the garden, letting you see it from different angles, surprising you at a turn. The path should lead somewhere — to a bench, a surprise object, a stunning plant, or a beatiful view.

Don't you just want to set off down this path and see what lies around the corner?

Even in a small garden, a path can meander through plantings, making the area seem larger than it really is, and linking the various elements. A straight path, especially in a small garden, leaves nothing to the imagination: it is all there, laid out before you, giving you no reason to explore.

On longer paths, offer places to stop and reflect or observe. Benches placed along the length allow the visitor (or weary gardener) to sit for a few moments and see the garden from a different angle.

FOCAL POINT

A focal point is an item — a special plant, a structure, a piece of furniture, a statue, a birdbath — that draws the eye and makes you want to get nearer to it. Generally, it is located at the far end of the yard, but a well-landscaped yard, even a small one, can have two non-competing focal points.

Use plant material as a focal point. If you have an existing tree in your garden that has qualities that make it worth keeping, you have a ready-made

A focal point with a sense of mystery, partially shrouded in greenery.

focal point. Trees that have a lovely shape, interesting bark and leaves, and are attractive all year long can be the point around which your whole garden revolves. A bench placed at its base can help draw attention to it.

Focal points can be used to help create optical illusions. A focal point placed on the sight line from a window to the furthest point of the yard will make the yard seem longer — the focal point draws the eye and directly behind the object is the place where the garden is at its maximum length.

COLOUR

Colour is such an important aspect of garden design that I will devote the entire next chapter to it, but let's just touch on a few thoughts here. Playing with colour in the garden is great fun, and it is easy to get carried away with so many lovely flowers to provide colour in your garden. Some restraint is necessary, especially if your desire is to use the garden as a place of peace and relaxation. Reds, oranges, and bright yellows are considered "hot" colours and are thus stimulating; whites, blues, pinks, lavenders, and pale yellows are cooler and are more relaxing.

Experiment with colour. Gardening is a forgiving hobby and a plant that clashes can be moved to another spot in the garden or given to a friend.

TEXTURE

Texture in the garden refers to many things — the ground cover (grass or some other plant); the material of paths and decks; the background material (plants, walls, fences, etc.); the foliage and type of flowers of the plants.

As a good example of the variety of texture in the plant world, think of the family of hostas. With over 300 varieties to choose from, hostas can provide a great range of textures and colours, depending on the varieties you plant — foliage that is puckered green-blue, ribbed deep blue, glossy shiny green with yellow margins, ice-blue and lance-shaped, and many mat finishes. Such plants grab your attention.

Fine-textured plants, such as maidenhair fern, seem to recede from view. They may look smaller than they really are, so use them in a small area to help make it look bigger and more restful.

Another aspect of texture is what is left when the leaves of the plant fall or die. Although leaves may be fine-textured and lacy, such as a cutleaf sumac's, the bare trunks and limbs are thick, coarse, and rough.

Most plants fall between the two extremes of bold and fine textures. As with so much else, finding that right balance is a challenge — too many

A classic example of contrasting textures and shapes at work: the delicate fern against the round, solid leaf of wild ginger.

varied textures and the effect is jumbled, busy, and jarring; too much sameness, and the effect is boring and lifeless. Assess the plants you want to use together in a bed or setting. Consider their overall shape, the shapes of the leaves, the mature height and spread. If your border is a perennial one, texture becomes an important consideration. Most perennials have a rather short flowering period, but their foliage will be on display for the whole season.

Consider too the texture of your furnishings — the decks, paths, fences, containers, benches, tables.

BALANCE: SYMMETRY AND ASYMMETRY

Whether it is the design for a garden, a building, or even a book, the designer thinks about balance. Symmetrical balance occurs when one half of an object is the mirror image of the other half. Asymmetrical balance is a somewhat more complex concept. Instead of using matching items to give a feeling of balance, balance is achieved by offsetting one thing against another. For example, a symmetrical arrangement involving a bench would have the bench flanked by containers of equal size containing the same type of plant or arrangement. An asymmetrical setting would have the bench flanked by a large container with a leafy plant at one end and a grouping of three or four pots of smaller plants at the other. Or perhaps an upright shape has a low mound as its counterpoint. These opposing shapes, sizes, or textures provide the design with tension and make it livelier.

Don't look for a balance or opposite for every single item in the garden, however. Other plants can be used as links for these balancing items and can provide a calming background for them. Achieving balance is not a matter of tit for tat — for every glossy-leaved plant, you must have a mat one. Rather, it is balancing groups of plantings or other objects.

Attempting to achieve balance by using asymmetrical plantings and arrangements can sometimes result in a lopsided look. How can you avoid this? As you look at the scene that bothers you, imagine that you can give the main elements a weight. If you placed these elements on a scale, would they balance? If not, your asymmetrical arrangement isn't truly asymmetrical — it's lopsided. For example, a tall pyramidal Japanese yew is equal to three rounded dwarf Japanese hollies — the volume of the three hollies is equal to the volume of the yew. If you want a more open plant to balance the hollies, you would need more of them because the "visual weight" of each open

The visual weight of the taller evergreen and the shorter rounder one is equal.

plant is less than the visual weight of each denser holly. You don't always need to achieve balance through size; for example, you could balance a large plant with one that has a bright colour.

HARMONY AND CONTRAST

Closely related to balance is harmony — the idea that things should go together in a pleasing and peaceful fashion. Harmony is not the same thing as sameness. Some gardeners are instantly attracted to plants with delicate ferny leaves and graceful nodding flowerheads — cosmos, flax, 'Moonbeam' coreopsis; others might like the bold foliage of yucca or hosta. But if the garden is full of plants with these features, it can become boring or exhausting.

Strangely enough, contrast can bring about a harmonious feeling. As with balance, each element should have something to offset it — a foil. By all means, keep an abundance of feathery-leaved flowers, but balance them with the contrasting leaves of the hosta or the rigid blades of the iris's foliage. Match mounding mats with upright clumps. In the next chapter, on colour, you'll see how to use colour in the same way — to suddenly introduce a contrast or foil to brighten and enliven the whole picture.

When you are looking for these contrasts to provide harmony, keep in mind that the plants must desire the same growing conditions.

In the flowerbed, group after group of flowering perennials and annuals can become quite tedious. Use foliage plants to break up expanses of colour that can tire the eye, or plan the border so that the foliage of the peony, for example, can off-set a late-blooming perennial. Plants with silver foliage are especially valuable in the garden for they mix well with hot or cool colours. Grasses can be used to make a transition from one colour scheme to another and to vary height and texture in the border.

If using plants as contrast is not to your liking, set objects, such as stones or boulders, by a path or at the edge of a planting of similar shrubs. A piece of statuary set among plants of similar habit or colour can offer all the change that is needed.

SHAPE

Plant shape, especially of trees and shrubs since they are so visible all year long, is another important part of design. Plant shapes have been divided into seven classifications: columnar (sometimes called fastigate), pyramidal (sometimes called conical), round, spreading (sometimes called horizontal), vase-shaped, weeping, and irregular.

COLUMNAR: narrow, upright shapes; attract attention in the way a steeple can stand out from other roofs; leads the eye up; creates an uplifting feeling; use with caution as it is a strong focal point; too many, especially scattered about, will look overdone; used in a line they are stiff and formal; make a good counterpoint to lower rounded or spreading plants. Examples: columnar maple, juniper.

PYRAMIDAL: broad bases, narrow or pointed tops; point upward but are not as severe as columnar forms; visually heavy and formal; use with restraint as accents; sloping lines look good with sloping roof lines. Examples: spruce, fir, yews, pyramidal oak.

ROUNDED: can be almost perfectly round or rounded on top; neutral, easy-to-get-along-with shape; make good fillers and work well with other shapes. Examples: winged euonymus, red oak, mugho pine, globe cedar, boxwood.

SPREADING: grow wider than they are tall; have horizontal or nearly horizontal branches; use to emphasize other horizontal lines in landscape; carry the eye across a design, making it appear wider than it is; good companions for columnar and pyramidal shapes. Example: spreading juniper, cotoneaster.

VASE-SHAPED: narrow bottom, arching top; provides graceful note to garden; often have space beneath branches for other plantings; are especially good for street plantings and small gardens. Examples: Japanese flowering cherry, magnolia, skyline locust.

WEEPING: branches grow in a drooping fashion, sometimes right to the ground; good on slopes and hillsides where they can spill down. Examples: weeping willow, weeping caragana, weeping mulberry.

IRREGULAR: often described as picturesque, craggy, rugged; branches are held in uneven tiers; look good in silhouette in naturalistic sites. Example: European larch (at maturity), corkscrew hazel, Japanese maple.

Keep the shapes of large trees and shrubs uncluttered. Don't plant shapes nearby that will interfere or compete. Weeping trees, for example, should be given plenty of room to show off their pendulous branches and look best with plants that are low and horizontal.

Choose a tall plant as the focal point in a planting and surround it with plants of lower growth habit and complementary shape. For example, rounded dwarf shrubs can be tucked under the arching branches of a vase-shaped tree. They will fill without competing against the larger tree's shape or interfere with its growth.

SCALE

Another important consideration is the scale of the elements in the garden. Do flowerbeds seem too big or small in relation to the size of your property and house? Are delicate foundation plantings lost against the large sweep of brick that is the front of your house? These are problems of scale.

Scale is relative. There is no way of deciding in absolute terms what is too big or too small, but here are some handy guidelines.

❋ ....

The total depth of your borders should equal one half the width of the lawn. The half can be divided

Planting Distances
Shrubs: *Add mature height of A and B. Divide by three to give planting distance apart.*
Trees: *Add mature height of A and B. Divide by two to give planting distance apart.*

SHRUB A

SHRUB B

TREE A

TREE B

into further halves if you want a border on each side of the lawn.

Make freestanding (island) beds half as wide as the distance from which you will be viewing them most frequently. If your sitting area is 6 m (20 feet) from the bed, make the bed no more than 3 m (10 feet) wide.

REPETITION AND RHYTHM

Give a sense of unity to your design by using repetition of colour, shape, texture, or plant. This can be a difficult thing to do if you are eager to use as many plants as possible, but if you are interested in creating a feeling of relaxation and peacefulness, this is a good principle to employ. In the section below on designing the flowerbeds, I talk about planting in drifts, which is a perfect way to introduce some simple repetition into your bed. As you plan out the drifts, repeat some of the plants further down the bed. You will be amazed at the wonderful rhythmic effect this has.

A somewhat more sophisticated and difficult type of repetition is that of shape. Imagine that you have clipped a box or yew into a rounded shape and it is growing in a container. Nearby, you might set a gazing globe in a flowerbed; along the front of the bed plant a plant that has a rather rounded growth habit — lady's mantle or pinks.

A rhythmic pattern that is evident in the winter can be created by planting groups of heavy and light large plants — trees and shrubs — throughout the landscape. Balance is important at all seasons of the year. Dense evergreens should be offset by masses of deciduous shrubs so that the evergreens are not too overwhelming and sombre.

In the top illustration, the evergreen blocks a window and the other plantings are spotty, with no feeling of unity. In the bottom illustration, two delicate trees — possibly a honey locust and a white birch — frame the house, softening the hard edges. The foundation plantings are grouped nearer to the house, where they make a nice transition from the house to the lawn and bring attention to the front entry.

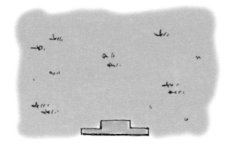

An unobstructed, panoramic view

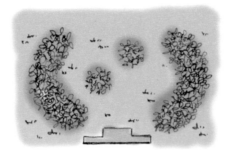

Masking the view slightly to bring viewer into the garden

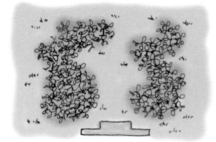

Restricting the view even more

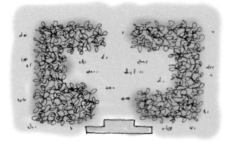

Symmetrical planting formalizes the view

TREATMENT OF A VIEW

If you are fortunate enough to have a wonderful view from some part of your garden, you do not want your plan to either ignore it or obscure it. Decide what you want the view to do for you. Do you want to see it when you sit out on your patio? Is it a view you want to tempt the visitor to see? Put yourself in the spot from where it will be viewed when you start to design the way you will emphasize or frame it.

FRAMING

The front of your house may be a problem. Someone — not you! — has planted an evergreen right in the middle of the front lawn. Now it has grown up and is blocking light from the house. At the corners of the house and on either side of the garage door may be small shrubs or evergreens. Somehow it just doesn't hang together. Instead of proudly occupying the centre, the house is trying to fight all the other elements.

Look at your house as if it were the main feature in a painting. The plant material should act as a frame for the house. In your mind, set off to one side a smaller evergreen, with a hedge up one side of the drive. Now you can fill in other parts of the plantings — perhaps a well-placed shade tree at the side yard — but none of them should outrank the framing plants. Apply this idea to other parts of the garden, especially when dealing with focal points, a lovely view, or any feature you want to emphasize.

DESIGN CONSIDERATIONS

USE AND PLACEMENT OF TREES

The first thing you will likely notice about your garden is the presence or absence of trees. The placement of a tree is often what guides the design for the rest of the garden. So the first step is to decide what trees stay, what trees go, and what trees should be added.

After a full year in your home, you will now have seen that tree through all its seasons. You will know how much shade it casts, what its branches look like in winter, whether it is in good health. You might also have pruned either it or the plants around it so that suddenly it becomes the star of the garden rather than the big problem. If, in the end, you decide it has to go — and sometimes this is the only answer — be sure that you are legally within your rights. If the tree is at the front of the house, it might be on municipal property and not yours to get rid of. Also, some municipalities have enacted bylaws regarding the size of tree that can be cut down.

Adding trees to a property has its own set of considerations. It is important to know the mature height and spread of the tree as you decide on its placement. You also have to know the purpose of the tree — to be a focal point, to block an unattractive view, to provide shade, to give privacy, to act as a windbreak, to provide fruit or berries. A new tree will take some years to meet these expectations. In the meantime, it is hard to imagine that the little sapling you have just planted may some day grow to be a giant. Fight every instinct to plant a sapling too close to the house. A tree that will have a spread of 12 m (40 feet) should be planted so that its trunk is at least 7 m (22 feet) from the nearest structure. In small urban gardens, this may seriously restrict the type of tree you plant. Many dwarf flowering trees are right at home in small spaces: serviceberry (rounded form, 9 m/30 feet); corkscrew willow (fabulous in the winter with its corkscrew-shaped branches against snow or a slate-grey sky; 3 m/18 feet). There are many mid-sized and dwarf evergreens, as well.

USE AND PLACEMENT OF SHRUBS

Shrubs, winter-hardy woody plants, can provide the background against which the rest of the garden is presented or they can be used on their own. Carefully chosen shrubs can offer delights of colour throughout the season. Keep in mind their eventual spread and height, as well as the colour combinations that will surround them.

Shrubs look best loosely arranged in groups. An exception is when the purpose is to make a hedge. In many urban gardens, however, there is not the space to design groves of small trees or shrubs, so you are usually going to be dealing

A form for every need: tall pyramidal, medium pyramidal, columnar, rounded, half-erect, and spreading.

A Common Landscape Problem

Top: *The evergreen has outgrown its yard. It breaks the line of the house, blocks the view, and shuts out light. The foundation shrubs are spotty.*

Bottom: *The house is framed with a lighter tree set off to one side. Foundation plantings extend for the full width of the house and the drive and front are clearly defined by a short hedge. A small tree between the house and garage makes a nice transition between the attached buildings.*

A Problem of Scale
Top: *Plantings soften the foundation but the small tree and shrub on the lawn, as well as the two evergreens at the side of the house, are lost and not in scale.*
Bottom: *The taller tree off to the side is in scale. The fence ties the house to its site and leads the visitor naturally to the front door.*

with single specimens. Choose one that can hold centre stage — for example, it should have dramatic foliage, masses of colourful flowers, or an appealing scent.

DESIGNING THE FLOWERBEDS

Flowerbeds have been with us for only about a hundred years, but it is hard to imagine a garden without them. There are several concerns you will run into when you start to think about flowerbeds:

- How big should they be?
- What shape should they be?
- What should be planted in them?
- Where should they go?

Let us take some of the design concepts I've been discussing and see how they apply to designing flowerbeds. Here are a few guidelines to follow as you think about the design of the beds and borders for your garden.

Generally, make beds as big as your space allows you, and that are in keeping with the scale of the rest of the garden and the landscape. Refer back to the discussion on scale for figuring out the size of flowerbeds. Be sure that you will be able to reach into the centre of a freestanding bed or the back of any border to easily tend the plants that are farthest away.

The shape should be whatever fits in with the design of your garden. If your style is fairly formal, straight lines and angles are appropriate; more casual designs look best with flowing lines.

Sketch out the shape and placement of flowerbeds or head out to the garden with some rope, a hose, or even a bag of flour — you are going to make outlines that you can move around or erase. Every now

Plan a background for the border, then add the flowers. Aim for a variety of heights, colour groupings, and textures.

and then, go back into the house to check the view from the windows.

❊

For easy-care mowing, use borders rather than freestanding beds. Freestanding beds take longer to mow around, especially if they are irregularly shaped, and they can make your yard feel small.

❊

Most flowerbeds run down one or both sides of a yard. You can also put a deep bed across the back of the property, especially if it is a long narrow lot. This will help make it seem wider. Of course, you might have to make small paths with stepping stones to allow you into the back if the bed is too deep to reach the plants at the rear.

❊

Flowerbeds can also be built out into the centre of the garden, perhaps joined by an arbour that takes you to the other part of the border. In effect, the flowerbeds have become "walls" that separate two garden rooms.

❊

In the end, it is your personal taste — and the needs of your plants, of course — that will dictate where the beds go and what shape they will be. Don't be afraid to be bold!

❀ When estimating how much you can plant in a bed, find out the mature spread of the plant and allow enough space to accommodate that spread. To create a lush effect, plant them a little closer than recommended — but leave enough room so that their growth will not be hindered. And if you have estimated incorrectly, plants can be moved!

❀ Large plants are best planted at the back of the bed, with mid-sized plants in the middle, and low-growing plants at the front. Use a range of heights.

❀ Plants with dense growth are better at the back of a bed; delicately shaped plants are better at the front of the border.

❀ Think in terms of mass colour. Too much variety in a bed can detract from the visual impact. Five marigolds will be far more impressive than two marigolds, a lamb's ears, and a veronica.

❀ Plant in drifts so that there is a flowing and relaxing feeling to the planting. It is easy to draw drifts on a garden plan — imagine a series of circles and ovals overlapping each other so that not one is complete. If you are planting a new bed, use a bit of flour to mark out similar shapes on the prepared soil. Then plant within those shapes. Keep in mind the colours that are complementary.

FOUNDATION PLANTINGS

Designing the plantings to go around the foundation of your house is one of the most challenging tasks facing you. In a new house, don't be in rush to plant. The earth around the new construction is still probably settling, so leave it for a year and use the time to assess what would be appropriate for your style of house. If the bare foundations really

Lush foundation plantings that take into account the architectural features of the house. The climbing rose moves the feeling of abundance up off the ground.

bother you, fill the area with container plants for the summer. Over the year, you will be able to see how well the overhang of the house protects the foundation area — and therefore how dry it will be.

When you are ready to plant, learn from other people's mistakes. Don't put in plants that will soon obscure your windows. If the site is dry, don't put in plants that require a lot of moisture. Try something other than evergreens and put in some small flowering shrubs, underplanted with bulbs for quick spring colour. The warmth from the wall will probably encourage them to get growing a bit more quickly than if they were farther away.

Refer back to the discussion on framing the "picture" and apply the principle to the foundation plantings. Their purpose is to eliminate the sqaureness of your house's exterior while complementing its architectural style.

Porches, Decks, and Patios

Places to sit, to eat, to entertain; places to offer protection from the weather or to enjoy the garden in spite of soggy soil and wet grass — porches, decks, and patios are useful for any number of reasons. In fact, decks are considered so necessary that many real estate listings now boast of decks with other features such as whirlpool tub and central air.

Porches offer the advantage of being covered, providing protection from heat, wind, and rain. But, they do not fit into every architectural style. A partially covered deck would be more appropriate for many of today's houses. Porches are often an addition to the front of the house, and are a reminder of days gone by when sitting on the front porch and chatting to neighbours was the way to spend hot summer evenings. If you are thinking of adding a porch to the front, match it carefully to the style of your house.

Decks usually lead off the back of a house, although they can be attached to the side of a house, depending on the layout. They serve a multitude of purposes: a play area, a place for the barbecue, for eating, for showing off potted plants, and so forth. They offer a firm hard surface for chairs and tables. Decks are easy and relatively inexpensive to build, although you can go all out and incorporate built-in seating areas and planters, as well as having several levels joined by stairs or walkways.

Decks are usually made of wood, but in areas with frequent rainfall, the wood can become slippery with algae. Wood can require some upkeep, but if left to weather, it will take on an attractive weathered appearance. New products on the market provide durability with easy care. One is a type of wood made from waste wood products. It fades to a pleasant soft grey and, although it can be painted, it can be left as is year after year with no rotting and no slivers! Pressure-treated lumber has been soaked in preservatives under heat and pressure. When working with this lumber, cut it outdoors and always wear a mask. Do not burn the scraps — and don't put the sawdust in the compost. Most pressure-treated lumber is softwoods such as fir and pine, which weather to a silvery grey. Redwood is expensive but resists rot and is therefore longlasting. If unpainted, it will weather to an appealing brown-grey. Cedar is strong, lightweight, rot-resistant, and less expensive than redwood. It weathers to a silver grey if not treated with a sealer.

For houses built before the fifties, a patio or terrace is a better alternative for fitting in with the architecture of the house — although a patio is appropriate for nearly any type of house. A brick or stone patio can have an elegance lacking in a wooden deck or porch. If plants such as moss or thyme are tucked between the cracks, a soft effect is achieved, making a nice blending of the hardness of the stone with the softness of the plant material. A local stone is most appropriate as it fits in with the landscape. If brick is chosen, be sure that it is durable and will withstand your weather conditions. Interlocking paving stones are guaranteed to stand up to our contrary weather — intense heat, cold, snow, rain — and come out smiling. They are available in many colours, textures, and shapes.

If privacy is important for the deck or patio, add trellises, plantings, or fences to screen out the sight lines from the street or neighbours' windows or gardens.

SHEDS

The dream of every gardener is to have a place to store all the paraphernalia that goes with gardening — and how we love to accumulate it! Just a little place is all we ask, a place for our seeds, potting soil, pots, rakes, hoes, lawnmower, watering cans, spreaders, bags of fertilizer and peat moss, sieves, hats, gloves, wheelbarrow, and if we could just have a place to sit and read our gardening catalogues and books ... it is easy to get carried away, isn't it? Perhaps you can't have a shed that will have room for everything I've listed above, but even the smallest shed can hold a surprising amount of equipment.

The utilitarian metal shed is easy and fast to install but it is not always particularly attractive. If you have one of these sheds, refer back to the discussion on rooms for some ideas about how to hide it. If you are going to have a shed built, here are a few thoughts:

❀ The design and materials with which it is built should be similar to your house.

❀ Can it be attached to an existing structure, such as the garage, to minimize the effect it will have on the landscape? If your house is undergoing renovations, perhaps a structure that performs the functions of a shed can be attached to the new addition. Check your municipality's bylaws before building anything.

❀ ....

If the utilitarian nature of the shed can be concealed by an attractive design, consider using the shed to separate parts of the garden. Build or place a small bench on the side that faces the ornamental garden, for example, to create a sunny spot to relax in; or use that wall to attach a trellis and plant a rambling rose.

SOME DESIGN AND PLANTING TIPS

Here are a few tips that might help as you design or redesign your garden. In fact, as you read through them, you might decide that your garden doesn't need a complete overhaul, just some judicious planting and pruning.

❀ ....

Ferns, with their delicate foliage, make a good job of softening hard landscape features and straight lines if planted close to the edge of a path. Their fronds are shown to great advantage when planted in a rocky outcropping.

Lilies make a wonderful addition to the border. Not only are they heavily scented, they add height and another texture with their foliage.

❀ Alpine plants will soften rocks and boulders and usually prefer the type of soil where these features are found.

❀ Scented plants will release their perfume if placed near a path where they can be brushed; place some near windows and doors so the scent can waft into the house.

❀ Brighten up a dark corner of the garden with a silver-leaved plant, such as artemisia.

❀ Plant deciduous shrubs in front of an evergreen background to anchor them to the landscape during the winter months.

COLOUR

· ·

More than anything, gardening is about colour — bright dazzling reds, soft romantic pinks, calming cool greys and lavenders — the array is almost endless. But how can you use colour to your best advantage?

Using colour well in the garden is partly a matter of trial and error — in other words, experience. It certainly helps to have an artistic eye but even if you feel like a klutz when it comes to deciding which colours go together best, you can learn some fundamental principles of colour. Soon, you will be able to put together wonderfully pleasing colour groupings in your garden, almost without thinking about it.

Just as I advised you to look at plants and other furnishings for their textures, so should you look at plants for their colours. What you will find is fascinating. The white petunia contains tracings of green, or pink, or yellow. Then there is the rose. "Red" doesn't begin to do justice to the array of shadings and variations you will find in one single bloom. Look at an iris or a pansy — who would have thought such complex variety of tints and hues could exist in such a small space?

Part of the colour in your garden has already been provided for you — the greens of grass and

A peaceful feeling from a beautiful soft pink rose.

foliage; the browns of trunk and stem; and the blue of the sky. Of course, foliage isn't always just green. It is green-blue, green-grey, silver-grey, yellow, even purple or pinkish. The same is true of brown and blue. The sky in the country near Saskatoon is a different blue than the sky over Halifax or Trois-Rivières. Even in those places, the blue changes from the bright clear sun of a summer day, to the steel grey of an impending storm, to the soft yellow-orange-pink wash of a setting sun. All these changes affect colour in your garden. Bright sun can wash out pale colours and overcast skies can brighten them, intensifying pastels and light colours. Bright sun can also intensify bright colours and make them richer. In shade, pastel pinks, lavenders, and yellows can seem to glow, but burgundy, purple, and other dark shades fade into the gloom. Let's enter the world of colour and learn more about using it in the garden.

The Colour Wheel

The colour wheel is a handy method of classifying types of colours. If you can handle colour well, if people compliment you on your combinations, you have a built-in understanding of colour. Whether you are confident, feel a bit nervous, or are completely overwhelmed by colour — understanding the colour wheel can help. It can confirm your instincts; it can suggest new combinations; and it can get you started confidently designing your beds and planning for your furnishings. Although I will be referring mainly to plant material as I discuss colour, remember that there are fences, walls of houses and garages, decks, paths, and so forth, all with their own colours. Don't forget to include them in your colour planning.

❋ **Primary colours:** Red, yellow, and blue are the primary colours. They are the basis for all other colours and are pure, lively, primitive, and demanding. Plant combinations of the primary colours and white are a knock-out.

❋ **Secondary colours:** Green, violet, orange. Each is a half-and-half mix of two primary colours. Green is equal portions of yellow and blue. Violet is equal portions of red and blue. Orange is equal portions of red and yellow. They are unsophisticated, fresh, happy colours. Plant combinations of secondary colours are quite dazzling.

❋ We now add another group of colours, called intermediate colours. They are obtained by mixing adjacent primary and secondary colours equally. Thus, yellow and orange give yellow-orange; orange and red give red-orange; the other intermediate colours are red-violet, blue-violet, blue-green, and yellow-green. We now have twelve colours in the basic colour wheel.

The colour of something is determined by the percentage of primary colours and black and white that have gone into its makeup, so it is not surprising that we each see gradations of colour slightly differently. What role do white and black play? White mixed with any colour gives a pastel version of that colour, called a tint. Black mixed in gives a darker colour and is called a shade. Black and white mixed together result in grey and when grey is added to a colour, the colour is a tone. These tints, shades, and tones are the colours that are of most interest to gardeners as few colours in nature are primary.

COMPLEMENTARY AND HARMONIOUS COLOURS

Complementary colours are any two colours *opposite* each other on the colour wheel. For example,

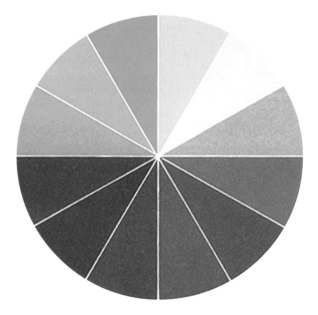

Refer to the colour wheel as you make your plant choices.

yellow and violet are complementary colours, as are blue and orange and blue-violet and yellow-orange. These combinations are classic, vibrant, and pleasing. If the pure colours seem too strong, use them sparingly or use tints or tones — peach with blue, lavender with pale yellow.

Harmonious colours — also called analogous colours — are those that merge into each other in the colour wheel. Yellow, yellow-green, and green, therefore, are harmonious and can be used to give a soft, subtle, soothing, peaceful effect..

THE EFFECT OF COLOUR

The colours you use in your garden will have a profound effect on the feeling or mood of the garden. First, you will choose colours you like — after all, the primary purpose of the garden is to please you! As time goes by, however, you might realize that you have too many hot reds or brassy yellows, even though you love their brightness and cheerfulness. It is now time to introduce a colour like blue to calm things down a bit, even if blue isn't one of your favourites.

In the garden, blues, lavenders, and greys give a cool misty feeling, an aura of romance. Cool colours, which include green, blue-green, blue, blue-violet, violet, and red-violet, seem to be farther away than they really are. However, too far away and they can seem weak and hard to see. Yellow seems to bring sunshine with it, even on a cloudy day. This is one of the reasons, I think, that it is such a popular spring colour (daffodils, forsythia, pansies, tulips, crocuses). Hot colours — red, red-orange, orange, yellow-orange, yellow, and yellow-green — seem to be closer than they really are and are easy to see from a distance. Bright yellows and oranges can be difficult to incorporate with other colours, but some lovely effects are achieved by mixing in some white and purple. Imagine bright yellow and orange marigolds growing out of a mix of purple and white alyssum — beautiful!

Additionally, each colour has its warm and cool variants. This depends on how much yellow or blue are in the colour. Let's look at two reds: scarlet and magenta. The red of scarlet is orange-red with a little yellow added to the red, making it a hot red. Magenta is made up of red with a little blue, making it a cool red. You can see the pitfalls you can get into when you talk only of red, or blue, or green!

CHOOSING COLOURS

Colour schemes can be broken down into four types: monochromatic, which uses a single colour as the foundation for all plantings; the cameo effect, which uses different tones of one colour and ranges into the colours closely allied to it; harmony, achieved by using simple colour combinations such as blue and white; and contrasting, using complementary colours.

MONOCHROMATIC: Not easy to carry off successfully, but stunning when done well. The most famous monochromatic garden is the white garden created by Vita Sackville-West at Sissinghurst Castle, in Kent, England. White in flowers, like many other colours, is quite complex: pure white, pinkish white, bluish white, silvery white, and cream are only a few of the many variations and they are not always good mates. Red is an especially difficult colour to match with other reds, but on a small scale it could be fun to try your own mini version of Sissinghurst — but don't confine yourself to white. Make a green bed, or a violet bed as an experiment. Practise with annuals for your monochromatic garden if you don't want to go to the expense of perennials. Introduce variety into the monochromatic garden by looking for variety in shape and texture. Small gardens, in particular, can benefit from the monochromatic colour scheme; it helps you resist the urge to cram too many colours into too small a space. The last part of this chapter is made up of plant suggestions for monochromatic gardens — it is also a good section to refer to when you are planning any of the other types of colour schemes.

CAMEO: An easier colour scheme to put together; could be described as the step before the monochromatic scheme. Choose a "foundation" colour — a bluish pink, for example — then, using the colour wheel, select plants with colours the foundation plant is related to.

HARMONIZING: The easiest and most personal of all colour schemes. Simply choose a colour combination,

A range of colours within the Sweet William family.

such as pink and white, or yellow, white, and burgundy. Use one of the colours — here's where white or grey prove their value — to separate the different shades, tints, and tones in the planting. If you have trouble deciding on which colours to choose for this type of colour scheme, take a look at a favourite flower. For example, look at a pansy. There are usually two, sometimes three, colours on its flower. There's your colour scheme! Harmonizing also allows you to use many colours in the garden because you can progress from cool creams to brighter yellows, on to warm reds, oranges, purples, and blues.

CONTRASTING: Similar to harmony, but rather more difficult to achieve a successful mixture. The challenge in using contrasting colours is that they tend to produce bold combinations — remember that the contrasting pairs are red and green, blue and orange, and yellow and purple (or violet). The effect can be lost in an overload of colour. But it is possible to come up with some breathtaking combinations — just use them with care. Blue and orange, for example, are contrasting colours that can make a lovely combination. Try blue delphinium with orange calendula or blue flax next to an orange-bronze marigold. Another way of making contrasting colours work is to use a paler tint of one of the colours. Contrast can also be used in a larger way: use hot strong colours in one part of the garden in contrast to pale cooler areas.

Thinking of the four types of colour schemes can help clarify the direction you want to take. You probably already have an idea of the feeling you want your garden to convey and recognize a natural inclination to go for either the hot or cool colours. Use the hot-cool concept and the colour schemes to focus on how you will achieve your vision. As well, take inspiration from what you see around you. Mother Nature breaks many colour "rules" and gets away with it. You will probably be happier, however, to start out with some tried and true combinations based on the colour wheel.

If you have decided on any garden except the contrasting one, keep in mind the idea of complementary colours (the contrasting garden is already made up of complementary colours). If your blue-based garden, once in bloom, seems to be lacking some life, tuck in a few orange marigolds. You will see a big difference. If your garden is too hot, cool it down with a few blue pansies.

USING COLOUR

A soft colour planted far from the house or sitting area will make the garden seem larger.

Bright colours planted just outside a window can make the room feel larger.

A harmonious colour scheme using bright colours.

❄ Plants with variegated leaves of white or silver are good in cool colour schemes. Variegated leaves of yellow or gold are best in warm colour schemes.

❄ Brighten up a dull corner with a potted white begonia or impatiens.

❄ Sharp contrasts, whether of colour or texture, arrest the eye as it travels along a bed; gentler contrasts keep the eye flowing.

❄ About a third of the border or bed should be made up of greenery that mingles with the other colours. The green can come from the leaves of flowering plants or specimens used solely for their foliage.

❄ As few as 30% of the flowers in a bed or border can be in flower at the same time to give a feeling of full flowering as long as they are distributed throughout the bed in drifts.

❄ Plant containers with plants of single colours. Observe how the colours look together then move the containers around the garden to see what other combinations work. When you see which colours are compatible, you will have the confidence to seek out and plant perennials and flowering shrubs with colours similar to your test plants.

❄ To tone down a strong colour, instead of using a neutral colour (cream, beige, tan, brown, silver, or grey), use a softer tint of the same colour. For example, the soft yellow of 'Moonbeam' coreopsis can tone down the clear primary yellow of sundrops.

❄ **GREEN:** Don't forget the value of green. It is easy to take it for granted because it seems to always be there. Green enhances all the other colours, but can be used to break up hot or cool areas or to act as a transition. Imagine trying to garden without the useful hosta — and think of all the greens it is available in! If you are undertaking a monochromatic colour scheme, the variations of green and its uses will become important to break up and link one shade and the next. In the listings in the section on monochromatic gardens, I have included a separate listing for green.

In the winter months and the late fall and early spring, green is one of the most important colours in the garden. Grass is often at its lushest in late November and early December, after drenchings of fall rain (in some parts of the country, of course, the grass is under snow by that time, and in others, the grass is green all year round). In the spring, the first green blades of grass are complemented by early bulbs pushing their green leaves above ground. The green of evergreens is with us all year, but it is never so important as during winter when its range — blues, greys, emeralds, yellows, dark, light — are more readily appreciated.

❋ ....

SILVER AND GREY: These colours have really come into their own over the past few years. The useful-

Use grasses for green or silver-grey notes or to make bold statements.

ness of silver or grey foliage is second only to white flowers, and they do the same thing. They quiet and cool a busy bright colour scheme and they act as links, or transition areas, to different colour schemes. They can also strengthen a plant's colour — especially mauve, lavender, or pale blue — that on its own doesn't have much impact.

Silver- or grey-leaved plants also have the advantage of usually being easy to grow, able to survive quite dry weather.

MONOCHROMATIC GARDENS

As much as possible I am guided by my sources about how I describe a plant's colour, but you might think of a certain plant as pink, for example, when I have said it is violet. I wouldn't worry about this too much; in fact, I think this is a sign that it could be a useful plant!

As much as possible, for your ease of use, I've put the plants in the broad colour category and tried to describe the colour as accurately as possible. Unfortunately, space is limited in a book such as this and you may find your favourite plant or colour has been omitted. I have tried to include colours which, in my opinion, are best suited for monochromatic gardens.

WHITE

A white garden gives an impression of space, as well as coolness and tranquillity. It is one of the easiest monochromatic gardens to assemble, for unlike many other colours, the different whites tend not to clash. As you study white plants, a new world opens up — white isn't just white any more.

It is white with a rose flush, or tracings of green, mauve, or yellow.

WHITE IN THE SMALL GARDEN

A white colour scheme makes a small garden seem larger. Put white-flowering plants against a hedge of dark evergreens or an ivy-covered fence. Grey- or silver-leaved plants have a place here. White annuals in pots can be moved around to give variety and to let you easily replace plants that have outlived their usefulness. Geraniums, petunias, pansies, and impatiens are popular annuals that grow well in pots. Variegated hostas and pachysandra will brighten shady areas. In the spring, snowdrops give an early white, and white varieties of crocus, hyacinth, and allium will continue it. Add dramatic white to the autumn garden with white varieties of flowering kale. Wrought-iron furniture will not overwhelm the small garden.

White for the autumn garden — flowering kale shows off one of the many shades of white.

Garden furnishings and decorations should maintain that sense of serenity, so choose dark greens and blues for paints and fabrics. Too much white used on tables, benches, and chairs may detract from the plants.

❀ **ASTER** (*Aster ericoides*): perennial; flowers in summer and fall; blossoms are white to pale blue; full sun to partial shade in well-drained soil; 30 cm to 120 cm (12 to 48 inches). Zone 3.

❀ **BELLFLOWER:** (*Campanula persicifolia* 'Alba'): perennial; flowers in spring and summer; blossoms are pure white; sun or partial shade in well-drained soil; 30 cm to 90 cm (1 to 3 feet). Zone 3.

❀ **CANDYTUFT** (*Iberis umbellata* 'Giant White Hyacinth'): annual; flowers all summer to well into fall; blossoms are snowy white; full sun in average soil; 20 cm to 40 cm (8 to 16 inches).

❀ **CLIMBING HYDRANGEA** (*Hydrangea petiolaris*): perennial climber; flowers late June to early July; blossoms are white, lacy, and scented; sun or shade, rich well-drained soil; 18 m to 24 m (60 to 80 feet). Zone 5.

❀ **CORAL BELLS** (*Heuchera × brizoides* 'White Cloud'): perennial; flowers in spring and summer; hundreds of small white blossoms; moist well-drained soil in sun or partial shade; 45 cm to 90 cm (18 to 36 inches). Zone 3.

❀ **DELPHINIUM** (*Delphinium grandiflorum* 'Album' or 'Galahad'): perennial; flowers late spring and summer; blossoms white; full sun for best results, rich, moist soil, dislikes acid soil; 1 m to 2.5 m (3 to 8 feet). Zone 3.

❀ **FOAM FLOWER** (*Tiarella cordifolia*): perennial; flowers in spring; blossoms are fuzzy white to pale pink; partial to full shade in humus-rich, slightly acidic, moist soil;15 cm to 25 cm (6 to 10 inches). Zone 3.

❀ **GOAT'S BEARD** (*Aruncus*): perennial; flowers in late spring and early summer; blossoms are white fuzzy plumes; moist soil in partial shade; 90 cm to 180 cm (3 to 6 feet). Zone 3.

❀ **LILY OF THE VALLEY** (*Convallaria majalis*): perennial; flowers in spring; blossoms are white and fragrant; can become invasive; sun or shade, in many types of soil; 20 cm (8 inches). Zone 3.

❀ **MOCK ORANGE** (*Philadelphus coronarius*): shrub; flowers in May to June; blossoms are creamy white and fragrant; full sun or light shade in well-drained soil; 3 m to 3.5 m (10 to 12 feet). Zone 3.

❀ **MOONFLOWER** (*Ipomoea alba*): annual twining climber; flowers all summer at night; blossoms large, white, and fragrant; full sun, rich porous soil; 2.5 m to 3 m (8 to 10 feet).

❀ **NICOTIANA** (*Nicotiana sylvestris*): annual; flowers from early summer to fall; blossoms are white and fragrant; partial shade, moist well-drained soil; 90 cm to 120 cm (3 to 4 feet).

❀ **PEONY** (*Paeonia lactiflora*): perennial; flowers spring to early summer; blossoms are white and some are white flecked with red depending on variety; full sun or light shade, on moist rich soil; 45 cm to 90 cm (18 to 36 inches). Zone 2.

❀ **SWEET PEAS** (*Lathyrus*): annual; flowers all summer, especially heat-resistant varieties; blossoms are creamy white ('Cream Southbourne), deep cream ('Lilly Langtry'), snow white ('Royal Wedding'), swan's down white ('White Supreme'); sun but some protection from midday sun is advisable, well-drained soil; 1.5 m to 4 m (5 to 6 feet).

❀ ....

THRIFT (*Armeria maritima* 'Alba'): perennial; flowers from early to midsummer; blossoms of this variety are white (other thrift varieties have vibrant pink, deep pink, or rosy-red flowers); full sun in average, well-drained soil; 25 cm to 35 cm (10 to 14 inches). Zone 3.

❀ ....

WHITE ROSES

- **'ICEBERG'**: Deservedly a best-seller; blossoms pure white; light green foliage; fragrant; repeat flowering; floribunda.

- **'BLANC DOUBLE DE COUBERT'**: Vigorous grower that makes a good hedge; blossoms pure white; deep green foliage; very fragrant; repeat flowering; shrub.

RED

Red is one of those colours that clashes with itself, depending on whether it is a red tending towards the blue or the orange part of the colour spectrum. An abundance of red flowers can be rather garish, so soften the effect with some white- and blue-grey flowering plants and silver- and grey-leaved foliage plants. Dark red and maroon will tone down sharp scarlets. For more reds than those listed below, look to coleus for red foliage, gladiolus, begonia, lily, zinnia, nasturtium, bearded iris, and chrysanthemum.

Rather than attempting to have a red garden from spring to fall, you might concentrate on a red theme for the fall, when brilliant reds and yellows are present in the landscape. The hot border created by an abundance of red will be less oppressive in the waning days of the season.

A safe colour for furnishings and accessories in the red garden is white or try dark green, red's contrasting colour, or a chocolatey brown.

Only Mother Nature can get away with this vibrant, glowing combination.

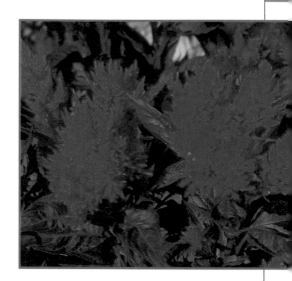

❋ **ASTILBE** (*Astilbe × arendsii*): perennial; flowers June and July; blossoms dark crimson ('Fanal'), warm creamy coral ('Rheinland'); partial shade, cool moist soil; 45 cm to 120 cm (18 to 48 inches). Zone 4.

❋ **BEEBALM** (*Monarda didyma*): perennial; blooms in summer; flowers are brilliant scarlet ('Cambridge Scarlet'), dark ruby red ('Mahogany'), red-violet ('Prairie Night'), reddish purple ('Violet Queen'); full sun to light shade, moist humus-rich soil; 60 cm to 120 cm (2 to 4 feet). Zone 4.

❋ **CARDINAL FLOWER** (*Lobelia cardinalis*): perennial; flowers summer and fall; blossoms are brilliant red; full sun to partial shade in constantly moist rich soil; 60 cm to 120 cm (2 to 4 feet). Zone 2.

❋ **CELOSIA** (*Celosia argentea plumosa*): annual; flowers midsummer to frost; blossoms bronzy red ('Apricot Brandy'), scarlet ('New Look'); full sun, rich well-drained soil; 25 cm to 60 cm (10 to 24 inches).

❋ **DAHLIA** (*Dahlia* 'Japanese Bishop'): flowers from August; blossoms are vivid orange-red with black centres; at least half day of full sun, well-drained soil; 90 cm (3 feet).

❋ ....

MALTESE CROSS (*Lychnis*): perennial; flowers in mid-summer; blossoms are brilliant scarlet (*L. chalcedonica*), orange-red (*L. × arkwrightii*), or magenta (*L. coronaria*); full sun to light shade in average, moist well-drained soil; 60 cm to 90 cm (2 to 3 feet). Zone 4.

❋ ....

PHLOX (*Phlox paniculata* 'Starfire'): perennial; flowers in spring and summer; blossoms are a vibrant deep red, foliage is red-tinged; 90 cm to 120 cm (3 to 4 feet). Zone 3.

❋ ....

POPPY (*Papaver orientale* 'Beauty of Livermore'): perennial; flowers in May to June; flowers are deep red; sunny well-drained spot; 60 cm to 90 cm (2 to 4 feet); Zone 2.

❋ ....

TRUMPET VINE (*Campsis radicans*): twining climber; flowers mid to late summer; blossoms are orange-red, attractive to hummingbirds; sunny spot, well-drained soil; 11 m (35 feet); Zone 4.

❋ ....

RED ROSES

- **'CRIMSON GLORY'**: Protect from noonday sun; blossoms deep crimson; glossy green foliage; richly perfumed; repeat flowering; hybrid tea.

- **'EVELYN FISON'**: Reliable and sturdy grower; blossoms scarlet; dark green glossy foliage; virtually no scent; repeat flowering; floribunda.

- **'FASHION'**: Has a long blooming season; blossoms coral; olive-green foliage; scented; repeat flowering; floribunda.

- **'VOGUE'**: Related to 'Fashion'; blossoms deep coral; grey-green glossy foliage; sweetly scented; repeat flowering; floribunda.

- **'SCARLET KNIGHT'**: Blossoms medium red; bright green leathery foliage; faintly scented; repeat flowering; grandiflora.

- **'Starfire'**: Tall and easy to grow; blossoms clear bright red; dark grey-green glossy foliage; no scent; repeat flowering; grandiflora.

- **'John Cabot'**: A great Canadian hardy climber that could also be grown as a shrub; blossoms deep red-pink; mid-green foliage; little fragrance; continuous flowering.

- **'William Baffin'**: Another famous Canadian Explorer rose. Hardy vigorous climber that makes a good hedge; blossoms medium red; mid-green foliage; little scent; continuous flowering.

YELLOW

Bright cheerful yellow, like red, can be a bit overwhelming unless thoughtfully planned. Yellow looks best in a sunny spot, tending to lose its brightness in the shade. By choosing yellows ranging from pale yellow all the way through to orange, you can put together a border that maintains its feeling of joy but is not too brassy.

An evergreen hedge is a good background, as is a white fence or wall. Furnishings in a yellow garden look best in pure white, light or dark green, or grey-blue. Accent flowers should be in the same range — white, sky-blue, or deep purple.

Other plants that flower in the yellow-orange range include snapdragons, coreopsis, primroses, wallflowers, poppies, and petunias. Remember to use foliage plants with yellow accents such as many of the evergreens, hostas, and euonymus.

BUTTERFLY WEED (*Asclepias tuberosa*): perennial; flowers in summer; blossoms are fiery orange, yellow, or red; full sun to light shade in average soil; 30 cm to 90 cm (1 to 3 feet). Zone 3.

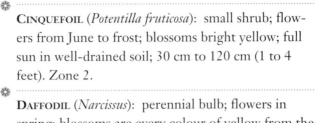

❀ **CINQUEFOIL** (*Potentilla fruticosa*): small shrub; flowers from June to frost; blossoms bright yellow; full sun in well-drained soil; 30 cm to 120 cm (1 to 4 feet). Zone 2.

❀ **DAFFODIL** (*Narcissus*): perennial bulb; flowers in spring; blossoms are every colour of yellow from the palest cream to the deepest gold; 10 cm to 45 cm (4 to 18 inches). Zone 5.

❀ **DAYLILY** (*Hemerocallis*): perennial; flowers from mid-summer; blossoms include colours such as glowing apricot ('Apricot Surprise'), red and yellow ('Fire Storm'), daffodil yellow ('King Alfred'), creamy yellow ('Going Places'); sun to part shade, well-drained soil; to 70 cm (28 inches). Zone 4.

❀ **FORSYTHIA** (*Forsythia*): shrub; flowers in early spring; blossoms are pale to bright yellow, depending on variety; 4 m (13 feet). Zone 5.

❀ **GEUM** (*Geum*): perennial; flowers in spring and early summer; blossoms are yellow-orange (*G. coccineum*

Heliopsis is a nice choice to introduce bright yellow to the garden. It is perfect for your cottage.

'Georgenberg'), bright yellow (*G. quellyon* 'Lady Stratheden'); full sun to light shade in well-drained but moist rich soil; 30 cm to 60 cm (1 to 2 feet). Zone 4.

GOLDENROD (*Solidago canadensis*): perennial; flowers in summer and fall; blossoms are bright yellow; full sun in average, well-drained soil; 60 cm to 150 cm (2 to 5 feet). Zone 3.

HONEYSUCKLE (*Lonicera japonica* 'Aureoreticulata'): vine; flowers in spring; blossoms white-yellow and fragrant; average garden soil; 9 m (30 feet). Zone 4.

JAPANESE KERRIA (*Kerria japonica*): shrub; flowers in April and May; blossoms are bright yellow; undemanding and tolerant of nearly any soil; 1 m to 2 m (3 to 6 feet). Zone 4.

MARIGOLD (*Tagetes*): annual; flowers all summer; blossoms from pale yellow to dark orange, depending on variety; 30 cm to 60 cm (1 to 2 feet).

YARROW (*Achillea*): perennial; flowers late spring to summer; blossoms are sulphur yellow ('Moonshine'); mustard yellow ('Cloth of Gold'), deep yellow ('Gold Plate'); full sun in average to poor well-drained soil; 90 cm to 120 cm (3 to 4 feet). Zone 3.

YELLOW ROSES

- **'PEACE':** One of the most popular roses; blossoms yellow edged with pink; green glossy foliage; slightly fragrant; blooms throughout summer; hybrid tea.

- **'CIRCUS':** Strong bushy plant; blossoms blend of yellow, salmon-pink, scarlet; semi-glossy deep green foliage; spicy fragrance; repeat flowering; floribunda.

- **'FRÜLINGSGOLD':** Easy-care hardy shrub; blossoms creamy yellow; light green foliage; scented; flowers in spring.

- **'HARISON'S YELLOW'**: Reputed to be the original "Yellow Rose of Texas"; blossoms gold yellow; mid-green foliage; scented; spring flowering.
- **'LEMON DELIGHT'**: blossoms clear yellow; mid-green glossy foliage; slight scent; repeat flowering; miniature.

BLUE AND PURPLE

One of the nicest combinations in the garden is blue and white, with some purple thrown in for good measure. Blues can fight with one another; for example, pure blues, as seen in gentians, and purple-blues, as seen in many campanulas, should never be mates. With the many blues available — far more than I have been able to even hint at here — the gardener who yearns for the cool calm of blue and white will not have trouble putting together a beautiful selection. Don't forget about those useful white and silver-grey plants if you are determined to have a wide variety of blues. Other transition plants can be white, or mass some green-foliaged plants to separate warring blues. Nice accents are provided by yellow, orange, or scarlet flowers introduced here and there.

Furnishings can pick up the colour themes mentioned above: woodwork can be light green, white, or yellow.

Other blues and purples are found in pansies, petunias, love-in-a-mist, anemones, and lavender.

❀ ....

BALLOON FLOWER (*Platycodon grandiflorus*): perennial; flowers in summer; blossoms are bright blue, violet-blue, clear blue, or rich blue, depending on variety, also in white or pale pink;

❀ ....

BORAGE (*Borago officinalis*): annual; flowers over the

Purple and white — a happy combination. A spot of yellow or red would add the finishing touch.

summer; blossoms are blue, purple, or white; average soil in full sun; 90 cm (3 feet).

BUGLEWEED (*Ajuga reptans*): perennial ground cover; spreads quickly in sun, slowly in shade. Zone 3.

BUTTERFLY BUSH (*Buddleia*): shrub; flowers in late summer to late fall; blossoms are purple or blue, as well as burgundy, pink, or white; well-drained fertile soil; 1.2 m to 4.5 m (4 to 15 feet). Zone 5

CLEMATIS (*Clematis*): perennial climber; flowering times vary; blossoms are a mauve-white-pink mixture (*C. alpina* 'Willy', flowers in May to June), purple (*C.* 'Jackmannii,' flowers June to July), indigo blue (*C.* × *durandii*, flowers July to September); sun to partial shade in acid-free soil; 2.5 m to 3 m (10 to 12 feet). Zone 2 for *C. alpina* 'Willy', Zone 4 for C. 'Jackmannii' and *C.* × *durandii*.

CORNFLOWER (*Centaurea*): annual; flowers all summer; blossoms are lavender, deep blue, or bright blue, depending on variety, as well as white, pink, or red; sun, in poor to average soils; 30 cm to 70 cm (12 to 28 inches).

❊ **CRANESBILL** (*Geranium*): perennial; flowers June to September, depending on variety; blossoms are blue ('Johnson's Blue'), as well as pink, white or violet, depending on variety; 30 cm to 45 cm (12 to 18 inches). Zone 4.

❊ **DELPHINIUM** (*Delphinium elatum*): perennial; flowers late spring and summer; blossoms dark blue ('Black Knight'), violet ('King Arthur'); full sun for best results, rich, moist soil, dislikes acid soil; 1 m to 2.5 m (3 to 8 feet). Zone 3.

❊ **FALSE BLUE INDIGO** (*Baptisia australis*): perennial; flowers May to June; blossoms are blue with blue-green foliage; ful sun to partial shade in average soil; 90 cm to 180 cm (3 to 6 feet). Zone 2.

❊ **FORGET-ME-NOTS** (*Myosotis*): self-seeding annual; flowers in spring; blossoms are bright blue or indigo blue, as well as white or pink; part shade in moist, well-drained soil; 17 cm to 30 cm (7 to 12 inches).

❊ **IRIS** (*Iris*): perennial; flowers spring and summer; blossoms are sky-blue (crested iris), blue-grey (stinking iris), deep blue to purple (reticulated iris), light violet (sweet iris); full sun to partial shade in well-drained soil; 15 cm to 90 cm (6 to 36 inches). Zone 3.

❊ **LARKSPUR** (*Consolida*): annual; flowers all summer; blossoms are every shade of purple and blue, as well as some pinks and reds; porous well-drained soil and full sun; 30 cm to 120 cm (1 to 4 feet).

❊ **MONKSHOOD** (*Aconitum napellus*): perennial; flowers August to October; blossoms are blue, violet-blue, lilac, as well as white, yellow, or cream; partial shade in cool, moisture-retentive soil; 60 cm to 180 cm (24 to 72 inches). Zone 2.

❊ **MORNING GLORY** (*Ipomoea*): annual climber; flowers all summer; blossoms are blue-purple (*I. purpurea*, *I. tri-*

Insects such as butterflies are attracted to bright colours. They bring another element of colour to the garden.

colour), rosy lavender (*I. tricolour* 'Wedding Bells'); average soil in full sun or light shade; 3 m (10 feet).

PINK

The pink garden or pink grouping of flowers seems to blend in naturally with plants bearing silver or grey foliage, but white, pale yellow, or lavender also have a place in the pink garden. Pink has an affinity for stone, whether it's a wall, path, or boulder that it is nestled against. Paint furnishings and garden accessories silver-grey, pure white, or Prussian blue to complement the rosy tones of the garden.

Pinks range from the palest blush to deep carmine. Needless to say, roses cover the spectrum of pinks, with delectable colours such as silvery-pink, salmon-pink, coral-pink, clear pink, and pearly pink. Annuals, such as geraniums, also come in a wide range of colours, among them various pinks such as orange-rose, salmon pink, coral pink, and blush pink.

Here is a list of a few plants with pink flowers, with information about their uses and cultivation.

❀ **ANEMONE** (*Anemone huphensis*): perennial; flowers in August and September; blossoms clear pink with golden eye; sun to part shade in moist humus-rich soil; 50 cm (20 inches). Zone 5.

❀ **AZALEA** (*Rhododendron mucronulatum*): shrub; flowers in spring; blossoms rosy-purple; moist partially shaded spot, acid soil; 1.5 m to 2.5 m (5 to 8 feet). Zone 5.

❀ **CLEMATIS** (*Clematis montana rubens*): perennial climber; flowers in June and July; blossoms are soft pink; sun to partial shade in acid-free soil; 2.5 m to 3 m (10 to 12 feet). Zone 5.

❀ **COSMOS** (*Cosmos*): annual; flowers summer to autumn; blossoms from pale pink to deepest pink (also in white, red, orange); average to poor soil in full sun; to 90 cm (36 inches).

❀ **HOLLYHOCK** (*Alcea rosea*): biennial; flowers in summer; blossoms blush pink to carmine (also yellow, white, deep red); full sun or partial shade, rich well-drained soil; 60 cm to 250 cm (2 to 8 feet). Zone 2.

❀ **MEADOWSWEET** (*Filipendula palmata* 'Kahome'): perennial; flowers in June and July; blossoms bright pink on crimson stems; sun to partial shade in moist soil; 100 cm (3.5 feet); Zone 3.

❀ **CREEPING PHLOX** (*Phlox subulata*): perennial; flowers in spring; blossoms are various shades of pink (also in blue or white); average well-drained soil in full sun; 10 cm to 20 cm (4 to 8 inches). Zone 3.

❀ **POPPY** (*Papaver orientale* 'Carneum'): perennial; flowers in May to June; blossoms are pink, salmon, flesh-coloured; sunny well-drained spot; 60 cm to 90 cm (2 to 4 feet). Zone 2.

RHODODENDRON (*Rhododendron carolinianum*): shrub; flowers in spring; blossoms pink-rose to lavender; part shade, acid soil; 90 cm to 180 cm (3 to 6 feet). Zone 5.

PINK ROSES

- **'SILVER JUBILEE'**: Makes good hedge or container plant; blossoms pink-apricot; green glossy foliage; slightly fragrant; repeat flowering; hybrid tea.

- **'SUPER STAR'**: Can be susceptible to mildew; blossoms pink-orange; green glossy foliage; fragrant; repeat flowering; hybrid tea.

- **'TIFFANY'**: Easy to grow; blossoms silvery-pink; olive-green foliage; fragrant; repeat flowering; hybrid tea.

- **'CAMELOT'**: Good cutting rose, blossoms coral-pink; glossy green foliage; spicy scent; repeat flowering; grandiflora.

- **'QUEEN ELIZABETH'**: Vigorous grower, sometimes classified as a floribunda; blossoms clear pink; large dark-green foliage; faintly fragrant; repeat flowering; grandiflora.

Colour and texture in one beautiful blossom.

- **'THÉRÈSE BUGNET':** Extremely hardy shrub; blossoms clear pink; red stems, medium green foliage; very fragrant; repeat flowering.
- **'DOROTHY PERKINS':** Popular rambler; blossoms pink; mid-green foliage; mild scent; flowers in summer.
- **'NEW DAWN':** Hardy rambler; blossoms soft pink; dark green foliage; scented; repeat flowering.
- **'DRESDEN DOLL':** Blossoms soft pink; glossy foliage; scented; repeat flowering; miniature.
- **'PEARL DE MONTSERRAT':** blossoms pearly pink; mid-green foliage; repeat flowering; miniature.

GREEN

For a truly monochromatic garden, there is nothing to beat the green garden. If you think it will be boring, liven it up with plants with variegated leaves and rely on texture and shape to provide the contrasts and interest. A topiary garden is the ultimate in a successful all-green garden. Here you can be guaranteed there will be lots of shape and texture. You can also be guaranteed there will be a lot of work involved, too!

A green garden is a natural at the cottage — ferns and grasses make an easy foundation from which to build. But the green garden can also be formal, with carefully clipped box emphasizing a symmetrical layout.

Garden furnishings should be white, deep brown, or deep green. Yellow or blue flowers can complement the plantings if you feel the need for a bit of colour — other than green. Here are a few green offerings.

BELLS OF IRELAND (*Moleculla laevis*): self-seeding

annual; flowers all summer; blossoms apple green, fading to a pale tan as they dry; sun or partial shade in rich, moist soil; 60 cm to 90 cm (2 to 3 feet).

BOXWOOD (*Buxus*): evergreen shrub; foliage is glossy green, responds well to clipping, and is slow-growing; rich soil in sun or part shade; heights vary according to variety. Zone 4, depending on variety.

ENGLISH IVY (*Hedera helix*): evergreen creeper/climber; lustrous dark green with white veins; rich moist and well-drained soil, full sun, where it will grow more profusely, to full shade; as vine, to 27 m (90 feet). Zone 4.

EUONYMUS: A large group of evergreen plants with shades from shiny dark green to light green, to variegated; leaves often change colour during the season. Useful in many situations; responds to clipping; tolerates many soil types. To Zone 3.

FERNS: Another large group, but valuable in any shady garden for the delicacy of their foliage.

LADY'S MANTLE (*Alchemilla mollis*): perennial; flowers in May and June; blossoms acid-green or chartreuse; foliage downy and grey-green — it has the bonus of catching water droplets that look like small pieces of mercury nestled on its leaves; sun or shade, soil must be well-drained but moist; 30 cm (1 foot). Zone 3.

SPURGE (*Euphorbia griffithii*): perennial; flowers in summer; blossoms are orange-red; foliage is pale green; full sun to partial shade, in well-drained, average to rich soil; 60 cm to 90 cm (2 to 3 feet). Zone 6.

SILVER AND GREY

These useful plants are some that can be used to make a tranquil garden, but use them for transition areas, too. They tend to prefer sunny areas. Here are a few to explore.

❈

ARTEMISIA: Valuable as a silver-foliaged perennial plant, many varieties in sizes from 30 cm to 120 cm (1 to 4 feet); noted for their long slender silver grey-white leaves; full sun, average well-drained soil. To Zone 2, depending on variety.

❈

DUSTY MILLER (*Senecio cineraria*): biennial; flowers in second summer; blossoms are insignificant, yellow or cream coloured; foliage is felty grey; sun, well-drained soil; 60 cm (2 feet).

❈

LAMB'S EARS (*Stachys byzantina*): perennial; flowers in spring and summer; blossoms are small pinky-grey; foliage is woolly and silver; average top rich moist well-drained soil in sun or partial shade; 15 cm to 35 cm (6 to 14 inches). Zone 4.

❈

LICORICE PLANT (*Helichrysum petiolatum*): grow as annual; furry leaves, grey on one side, silvery on the other; good in sunny exposed conditions, by the sea, and in containers where their arching, sprawling stems will spill over the edge; 90 cm (3 feet).

❈

PEARLY EVERLASTING (*Anaphalis margaritacea*): perennial; flowers in late summer; blossoms are papery white with yellow centres; foliage is grey-green; 30 cm to 90 cm (1 to 3 feet). Zone 3.

❈

RUSSIAN SAGE (*Perovskia atriplicifolia*): perennial; flowers July; small lavender blossoms; stems white, smoky grey pungent felty leaves; full sun, well-drained soil; 90 cm to 120 cm (3 to 4 feet). Zone 4.

❈

SANTOLINA (*Santolina chamaecyparissus*): perennial; flowers in July; blossoms are small, deep yellow, button-shaped; pale silver-grey foliage; average to poor soil in full sun; 30 cm to 60 cm (1 to 2 feet). Zone 5.

INDEX

See all 4 volumes in
The Complete Gardener series:

MARK CULLEN
THE COMPLETE GARDENER

COLOUR & DESIGN

Simplifies the process of design and demystifies the issue of colour. Essential information for planning your garden so it looks its best. Includes planting instructions on making your own all-white garden regardless of your garden size. Accompanied by video.

MARK CULLEN
THE COMPLETE GARDENER

FURNISHINGS

Learn how to add interest and charm through the furnishings in your garden. From arbours to urns—they're here! Features step-by-step directions for making and planting a "stone" trough that would cost a small fortune to buy! Accompanied by video.

MARK CULLEN
THE COMPLETE GARDENER

PLANTING & GROWING

These fundamentals of good gardening practice will help you to create and keep a garden full of blooming, healthy plants. Don't miss the recipe for compost tea—your plants will love it! Accompanied by video.

MARK CULLEN
THE COMPLETE GARDENER

PLANTS

Helps you select the best annuals, perennials, vines, ground covers, trees and shrubs and bulbs for your growing conditions. Special instructions on how to plant a beautiful four-season window box. Accompanied by video.